TRIUMPH

The extraordinary life and faith of
Louis Zamperini

JANET AND GEOFF BENGE

BroadStreet
PUBLISHING

Triumph: The Extraordinary Life and Faith of Louis Zamperini
By Janet and Geoff Benge

Published by BroadStreet Publishing Group, LLC
Racine, Wisconsin, USA
www.broadstreetpublishing.com

ISBN: 978-1424549122

Also published as *Louis Zamerpini: Redemption* by Emerald Books
The content of *Triumph: The Extraordinary Life and Faith of Louis Zamperini*
published under license from:
Emerald Books
P.O. Box 635
Lynnwood, WA 98046

Printed in the United States of America

To our own "Lucky Louie,"
Louis Ivan Kleinsteuber
our first grandchild,
born as we completed work on this book

CONTENTS

Chapter 1

THIS IS HOW IT ENDS?

L ouie Zamperini stood at the back of the cockpit chatting with pilot Allen Phillips (Phil) as he flew the B-24 Liberator bomber low over the Pacific. They were searching for a missing bomber that left Oahu, Hawaii, for Australia the day before and hadn't been heard from since. Louie and Phil scanned the ocean below as they talked, but they saw no sign of the missing airplane. Suddenly Louie felt a shudder. He looked to his left. Engine Number 1, on the far end of the wing, sputtered and shook, then stopped. Immediately the bomber began to tip left and lose altitude.

Louie stood back as Phil and copilot Charleton Cuppernell took charge of the situation. The propeller blades of the stalled engine needed to be feathered, turned blade edge to the airflow to reduce drag. Although feathering was normally the copilot's job, Phil and Charleton had switched seats during the flight so that Charleton could rack up flying hours in the captain's chair. Now the two men seemed out of sync as they responded to the emergency.

Phil yelled for their engineer to come feather the propeller blades. Louie made way as the rookie engineer raced forward, leaned across the instrument console, flipped open the plastic lid covering four buttons, and hit one of them. In a flash Louie realized the engineer had pressed the wrong button. He turned his head to see the Number 2 engine on the left side stop dead. The bomber's two left engines were now out. The plane, usually used only on short flights, could barely fly with four engines running, and Louie saw the shock on Phil's face as he increased power to the two right engines. Charleton frantically tried to restart engine Number 2. Louie grasped the bulkhead as the airplane spun wildly left and began to plummet toward the sea.

"Prepare to crash," Phil yelled into the intercom.

Louie leapt into action. Each crew member had a specific job to do at that moment. The bomber was fitted with two life rafts that would launch and inflate automatically after a crash. A third life raft was located in the bomb bay, and it was Louie's job to retrieve it. Louie grabbed the extra life raft, wrenched it loose from its housing, then dashed to the right waist window where he dropped to the deck beside the machine-gun mount. Louie took one last look at the sky from the waist window before tucking his head into his chest and pulling the uninflated life raft over him.

The bomber screamed toward the water, and with an ear-popping crash, Louie's world exploded. Louie saw daylight overhead before being flung forward as water engulfed him. He felt wires wrap around his torso, and in an instant he was facedown, wedged beneath the machine-gun mount.

Louie clawed at the wires wrapped around him like a giant nest of noodles, but he couldn't free himself. As the fuselage began to sink toward the seafloor seventeen hundred feet below, Louie gulped in salt water and gagged. He needed air, but there was none. He felt his lungs filling with water. *So this is how it ends? Nobody's going to live through this,* Louie thought. He wondered how long it would take the news of his death to reach his family and friends back home in

Torrance, California. Growing up there, he'd got himself into a lot of tight spots, but he always had a knack for finding a way out. The locals called him Lucky Louie as a result. Now, it seemed, his luck had run out. The mangled fuselage of the plane continued to sink, and Louie wished he were back in Torrance.

Chapter 2

A MAGNET FOR TROUBLE

Seven-year-old Louie Zamperini walked home from school with his head down, his eyes busily scanning the sidewalk for cigarette butts. When he spotted one, he swooped down and scooped it into a paper bag. Louie paid particular attention as he neared the main intersection in the small town of Torrance, California, where he lived. Intersections were gold mines of cigarette stubs. Louie had observed many people standing on the corner taking one last puff before throwing their cigarette to the ground and stepping off the curb. The area around the movie theater was another good source for butts. Louie also made sure to check the two hotels in town. Once he completed his usual circuit, he headed to a row of eucalyptus trees everyone referred to as Tree Row. Behind the trees was a drainage ditch with railroad tracks beyond.

Louie walked to the tenth tree from the left and reached into a hole in the trunk. He pulled out a small bag containing a pair of scissors and a few empty cans. The tins labeled Prince Albert Crimp Cut, Long Burning Pipe, and Cigarette Tobacco were worthless now, but when he had filled them with tobacco, Louie could sell the cans for a nickel apiece.

Louie sat beside the ditch and pulled out the paper bag of butts. He selected the longest one, put it to his lips, and lit it with a match. He sucked in the smoke before breathing out deeply. With the half-used cigarette dangling between his lips, Louie began cutting each cigarette butt open, allowing the tobacco to fall into the first Prince Albert tin. He kept at it until the tin was full and then moved on to filling the next tin. On a good afternoon Louie could fill two tins. At the movie theater on Saturday afternoons, he'd sell those tins of recycled tobacco to teenage boys for a nickel, half the price of a brand new tin of tobacco. When he finished filling the tins, Louie packed everything back into the bag and stuffed it into the hole in the tree before heading home.

On the way home Louie encountered several older boys from school.

"There goes the dago," one boy yelled, wheeling his bike around to face Louie.

Louie's body tensed. He hated being called a dago. He wasn't sure why people liked to pick on him. Perhaps it was his wiry, thick, black hair, his spindly legs, or his strong Italian accent. Even though Louie had been born in New York, his father and his mother's family were from Italy. Until Louie began attending school, he rarely heard English spoken either at home or in the neighborhood. Now, at school, he was learning to read and write in English, which he thought a strange language. The task seemed impossible. Already Louie was repeating first grade.

"Hey, wop, we're talking to you," another boy said as he rode his bike up beside Louie. Then another boy reached out and shoved Louie.

Louie yelled and flailed his arms, trying to fend off the boys as they formed a circle around him with their bikes.

"Best show in town!" one boy goaded.

While the comment made Louie angry, he'd grown used to such harassment. It happened all the time on the playground and going to and from school. The older boys picked on him, hoping to get him to swear at them in Italian.

When two of the boys got off their bikes and walked toward him, Louie slipped between two other bikes and took off running. Even though Louie was three or four years younger than the boys, he was sure he could escape his tormentors. Louie could outrun anyone he knew, except his older brother, Pete. Louie ran until he reached the railroad track and then ran along it, matching his stride with the railroad ties. He saw a small shed beside the track and ducked behind it. He looked back down the track. The boys were gone. He'd outrun them. It was safe to go home.

Keeping an eye out for more trouble, Louie walked past the Pacific Electrical Railroad Depot, where his father worked as a machinist. Louie's father had taken the job four years before, after the Zamperini family moved across the country from New York. Louie knew the story of their move well, and his mother liked to repeat it.

Louie, along with his father, Tony; mother, Louise; older brother, Pete; and younger sister, Sylvia, had lived in Olean, New York, before his next younger sister, Virginia, was born. Louie couldn't remember Olean, but his mother said the air there was cold and damp in winter. When both Louie and Pete came down with pneumonia, their parents asked the doctor what they should do. "The boys have weak lungs," he had said. "Take them to a better climate. I've heard California is warm and dry. That's where you should be."

Louie's mother's brothers, Nick and Louis Dossi, had already moved to San Pedro, California, and the Zamperini family decided to join them. Because the only way west for a poor family was by train, the Zamperinis had scraped together the money and purchased tickets.

Louise Zamperini always shook her head when telling the next part of the story. "I ushered the boys onto the train. Both were with me, and I had the bags and little Sylvia in my arms, as the train pulled out. Then I looked around and Toots (the family's nickname for Louie) wasn't with us. I yelled his name, but he wasn't there. I ran to the conductor and said, 'You have to back up. My Toots is left behind.' The conductor shook his head, but I kept yelling until he pulled the cord. The train rolled back down the tracks, and everyone looked out the windows for Toots. It was Pete who saw him walking along the track as if he didn't have a care in the world. He had run the whole length of the train and jumped from the caboose as the train gathered speed. I climbed down and scooped him up. He smiled at me and said, '*Sapevo che le sarebbe tornare*' (I knew you'd return for me)."

As he grew older, Louie began to wonder whether his parents secretly regretted returning to get him. Louie was like a magnet for trouble. Whenever something went wrong, he was in the middle of it.

By the time Louie was nine, the mothers on the street refused to let their children play with him after school. They said he was too tough, too angry, and too smart for his own good—street smart, that is.

Louie gathered a group of outcasts. He was their leader, and they called him the Brain because Louie loved thinking up ways to annoy people. The gang started with small projects. When Louie was the only boy in class not invited to a prissy girl's birthday party, he decided to go anyway—with his gang. It was too easy. While the partygoers were in the backyard playing games, Louie and his gang crept into the house, crawled under the table, hid behind the long tablecloth, and ate their way through all the party cupcakes. Afterward Louie led the gang outside. The boys hung out across the street, waiting to hear the commotion that would erupt when their deed was discovered. Louie found it satisfying to ruin other people's parties.

Louie soon learned about other things he could steal.

Every Saturday the Zamperini family drove eight miles south to San Pedro to buy their groceries and visit their uncles Louis and Nick. When Louie's relatives, along with a few other Italian families, got together, there was a lot of drinking, smoking, and storytelling about the old country. There was also lively music, with Louie's mother playing the violin and his father the guitar and mandolin. Although the making and selling of alcohol was prohibited in the United States, Uncle Louis always had an ample supply of wine and beer. No one asked where it came from. Hiding beneath the table one night, one by one Louie grabbed glasses of wine and drank them while the adults sang and told stories. Before long Louie was drunk. He stood on his wobbly legs, headed out the door, and collapsed into a nearby rosebush.

After that night, Louie began pilfering alcohol whenever he could. He also came up with a scheme to rack up money faster than he could selling used tobacco. He would rig pay telephones.

In the movie theater lobby was a row of pay phones, into which a nickel was inserted each time a person made a call. Louie layered toilet paper into the pay phone money slots and pushed it down so it couldn't be seen. Then a few times a day on the weekends, Louie secretly fed a piece of wire down the slot past the toilet paper and hooked the paper up. Along with it came all the backed-up nickels in the slot. It was easy money.

Louie often used this money to buy movie tickets. While he liked Charlie Chaplin movies, Westerns were his favorite. *The Man from Red Gulch, Riders of the Purple Sage, The Prairie Pirate, Tumbleweeds*—Louie watched them all. As he watched movie after movie, he yearned to be free like their cowboy characters, out on the wide-open plains with a horse and a gun. Louie fantasized about what it would be like to be free.

The idea of roaming free appealed to Louie, partly because he always felt like someone was poking his or her nose into his business. In third grade, his principal caught him smoking and beat him with a large leather strap. That night his father noticed the bruises on Louie's backside and asked what had happened. When Louie confessed, his father spanked him—on the same bruised spot. Despite the pain of the beating, Louie refused to cry. He was not a crybaby, and he would take like a man whatever punishment was meted out to him.

By his thirteenth birthday, on January 26, 1930, Louie was out of control. It didn't help that the country was in the grips of a crippling depression. Just months before, the stock market in New York had crashed, ruining many people financially and leading to large numbers of men being laid off from their jobs. Money had always been tight for the Zamperinis, but now, as the depression sent food prices skyrocketing, the family scrambled to feed themselves. Louie's mother fried stale bread, and she sent the girls out to gather wild mushrooms and berries, while Louie and Pete took their father's gun out to shoot rabbits and mud hens in the barley fields on the outskirts of town.

Although Prohibition remained in effect, there were ways around it, either by buying illegal liquor or by making one's own. Louie found a third way. He watched and listened until he knew which people in town made their own beer or wine. He would wait until Saturday night, when most people went to the movies. Louie and his gang would then break into people's houses and steal their alcohol supply. They hid the stolen bottles in an underground den Louie had dug in Tree Row. The growing pile of bottles made Louie smile. He knew his crime would never be reported to the police, since it was illegal to make alcoholic drinks in the first place.

Other "adventures" didn't end as well. When Louie stole some pies from a bakery truck, the driver reported him to the police, and Louie was forced to pay for the pies. This angered Louie, and he sought his revenge against the bakery truck driver. One night he saw the driver leaving the Torrance movie theater with a friend. Louie followed the young man and his friend down a dark street and then confronted them. The driver laughed, and Louie became incensed. He punched the friend, who fled. Then Louie started on the driver, punching and kicking the man until he collapsed and rolled unconscious into a ditch.

Louie was proud of how he had handled himself. He figured the driver would think twice before turning him in to the police again. However, in the early hours of the morning, Louie awoke in a cold sweat. He had beaten the young man mercilessly. What if he'd killed him? What if the man's body was still in the ditch? Fear gripped Louie as he thought about what he might have done. He had never considered that his actions could lead to the death of another person.

Early the next morning Louie returned to the scene of the beating. The young man was not lying in the ditch, although Louie didn't know whether that was good or bad news. Maybe the driver was alive and had left the scene. Or maybe the police had found the body, had removed it, and were now looking for the perpetrator. Two anxious days passed before Louie spotted the bakery truck driver, bruised and bandaged but alive. Louie let out a sigh of relief.

Soon after the beating of the bakery truck driver, the police arrived on the Zamperinis' doorstep. Louie knew it was serious when Chief Collier himself showed up.

"I want to borrow your son," the police chief told Louie's father.

No one had to ask which son. Louie's older brother, Pete, was a model son, a model student, and a model citizen. It was enough to make Louie sick to see how easy it was for his brother to get straight A's, invitations to the local parties, and good citizen awards at school.

"What's he done now?" Louie heard his father ask in a flat voice.

"Enough to land him in jail if we can get witnesses. Look, you're a good family. Let me take him for the afternoon and see if I can scare him straight."

"Louie, Louie!" Tony Zamperini yelled. "Come out here on the porch."

Louie waited a moment, then strolled out from around the side of the house.

"Go with Chief Collier," his father said.

Louie pretended to look surprised.

"Get in the car," the chief said.

Louie climbed into the 1929 black Model A Ford.

Neither Louie nor the police chief said a word as they drove through the streets of Torrance. They stopped outside the jail.

"Let's go inside," Chief Collier said.

The chief guided Louie through the jail, allowing him to get a good look at the prisoners in their cells. He stopped in front of a cell shared by two prisoners who stood at the bars staring.

"Where do you like to go on Saturdays?" Chief Collier asked.

"To the beach," replied Louie.

"Son, when you're in there, you can't go to the beach on Saturday or any other day. Truth is, Louie, if we didn't respect your folks so much, you'd be in reform school by now. This is a warning, son. Wise up, or this is where you'll end up."

Louie followed the chief back to the car for the drive home.

As Louie climbed out of the police car, Chief Collier said, "I hope you've learned your lesson."

Louie nodded. "Yes, sir, I have," he said, and he meant it.

Watching the black Model A disappear down the street, Louie had indeed learned a valuable lesson, just not the one Chief Collier had in mind. Instead he'd learned that the cops were on to him. If he was going to continue his life of crime and not get caught, Louie knew he would have to be smarter, much smarter.

Chapter 3

"YOU'RE ON THE TEAM NOW"

Louie waited in line at the hardware store to buy some canning jar lids for his mother. As usual, he eavesdropped on several conversations around him. His ears pricked up when he overheard the locksmith talking with a customer.

"I have a complaint," said an older man wearing a flannel shirt.

"What is it?" the locksmith asked.

"You sold me this lock and key last year, and I put it on my front door. Yesterday I pulled out the key to my son's house by mistake, and what do you know? It fit my lock. How's that possible? I thought keys were made for just one lock."

"I wish they were, sir," the locksmith replied. "Truth is, there are only about fifty different locks made in the United States. If you keep trying keys in locks, you have one chance in fifty a key will open any lock."

Louie's mind whirled. *One chance in fifty a key will open any lock!* How had he made it all the way to eighth grade without knowing this? This was a perfect way for Louie to be smarter at crime.

Over the next several weeks, as other students concentrated on their exams, Louie tried every key he could get his hands on in any lock he could find. He got lucky when he pushed the key to his back door into the rear door lock of the Torrance High School gymnasium. The lock turned, and the door swung open. *Too easy,* Louie thought. *Now to make some money.*

It took most of geometry class for Louie to figure out a plan. Admission to a basketball game at the gym cost ten cents. What if he offered to let students in the back door for five cents? Letting twenty kids in would make a dollar, just like that.

Louie didn't have to wait long to put his plan into action. A basketball game between Torrance High and their archrivals, Narbonne High, was scheduled that Saturday night. Louie's brother Pete, a senior, would be starting as center. Louie was secretly proud of Pete. The star athlete of the high school, Pete had made the varsity team in basketball, baseball, and track. He had already tied the United States half-mile high school running record and was aiming for the mile record in the spring. Louie couldn't understand Pete's attraction to sports. It seemed like so much work. Pete practiced day and night, with little time for fun. Worse, to be eligible to play on the teams, Pete had to keep his grades up. Louie knew sports weren't in his future.

The plan worked. Louie unlocked the gym's back door and let his gang and their friends in. Then he climbed into the bleachers to watch the game. As he looked at the crowd of fans, he felt proud that he'd found a way to make money off them.

Game after game, Louie "sold" cheap gym admission, until one night a teacher came to investigate where the stream of students entering from beneath the bleachers was coming from. When the teacher discovered Louie scooping nickels into his pocket, Louie's ruse was up. Despite being caught red-handed, Louie wasn't too concerned. What could the school do to him? Under Torrance Junior High's punishment system, every student started the school year with one hundred merit points. The principal called Louie into his office and explained that since he had already blown through all his merit points, fifteen points for this latest escapade would be deducted from his high school total. Louie would enter Torrance High in January with only eighty-five merit points left to lose for the year. He would also be barred from participating in high school sports, but Louie didn't care. What did it matter? He knew sports were not for him. Louie was just glad the principal didn't report him to the police this time.

Louie graduated from Torrance Junior High in December 1931. In California, children born during the winter months entered high school halfway through the traditional school year.

Christmas 1931 was hard. The depression was in full swing throughout the country. Louie knew that his father was lucky to have a job. Lots of other men did not. In fact, nearly 20 percent of men were looking for work, and some of the boys in Louie's class were not allowed to go on to high school, because they were needed to help provide food for their families.

In February 1932, Louie entered ninth grade at Torrance High, which shared the same campus with the junior high. On the first day, Louie discovered he was not banned from sports after all. Louie learned why when he mentioned it to Pete. Pete sheepishly explained that he had gone to see the principal, taking their mother with him. He had begged the principal to allow Louie to enter high school with a clean slate.

"Isn't that great?" Pete said. "Now you can do track with me."

Louie rolled his eyes. "You shouldn't have bothered," he muttered. "I'm not joining any team, ever!"

"You could if you wanted to. That's the point," Pete said, pressing the issue.

"Wild horses couldn't drag me onto the track," Louie said, imagining how embarrassing it would be to run in front of an audience. He was used to running away from trouble. He didn't see the point in running around a track with hundreds of people staring at you—watching you fail.

Louie's behavior had become antisocial. He refused to eat with the family, insisting instead on sitting on the kitchen floor and using the open oven door as his table. He also refused to sleep inside the house. At night he dragged his bedding outside and slept under the stars. Louie knew it was odd behavior, but that's what he wanted to do. What he did care about was hearing others talk about him. Louie hated that. He even overheard his mother talking to Uncle Louis and Aunt Margaret about him. "He's thirteen now," his mother said. "I think Louie's hair bothers him."

"His hair?" Aunt Margaret asked.

"His hair," his mother repeated. "Peter says Louie goes to bed with one of my old stockings on his head. He's trying to tame his hair, to fit in probably."

Louie's face burned at his mother's words. He hated that she knew that he was worried about his hair, which was thick and wiry and stuck out every which way. Most of the other kids in class had silky smooth hair, which Louie envied them. As far as he was concerned, there was nothing worse than dago hair.

Aunt Margaret took Louie aside and tried using hot irons to straighten his hair. She also encouraged him to use olive oil or pomade. Despite his aunt's best efforts, nothing helped Louie's hair.

By the end of February, Louie hated high school. Pete was a great student, an amazing athlete, and a natural leader—all things Louie's teachers soon learned Louie was not. It didn't help that the two brothers looked so much alike. "Chalk and cheese," Louie overheard his algebra teacher tell his English teacher. "There's no doubt those two Zamperini boys are as different as chalk and cheese." None of this made Louie want to try hard at school. He knew he couldn't live up to Pete's example.

At the end of February, the ninth-grade interclass track meet was to be held. Only four boys were in Louie's class, and the girls were determined that their class should win. They decided that Louie was their best chance in the boys' 660-yard race and asked him to participate. Louie refused. But the girls didn't give up. They sat with him at lunch, giggled at his jokes, and told him how good he'd look in the track uniform. Louie had never had so much attention—positive attention—in his life, and eventually he agreed to represent the class in the 660-yard race.

The race was an eye-opener. Louie got off to a poor start. He didn't want to mess with the ambitious boys who sprinted away from the starting line, but as they ran, he knew he couldn't catch up to them, either. At the end of the race, he was wheezing and came in dead last. Ashamed of his performance and hearing some of the girls laugh at him, Louie retreated beneath the bleachers, where he sat staring at the track and pondering what had gone wrong. Was running that difficult? Pete didn't make it seem so. The soles of Louie's feet throbbed, and Louie felt ridiculous. The race had been only 660 yards, a little over a third of a mile. Pete was working on setting a high school record for running the mile.

Louie considered the differences between him and his brother. Pete didn't drink alcohol every chance he got, nor did he smoke or try to do as little as he could to get by. Louie did all of those. He was sure he'd never race again. Changing all his bad habits just to run seemed far more effort than it was worth. Louie soon learned that Pete saw things differently.

"The first race is the hardest," Pete explained that night. "You'll never be last again if you let me help you train."

"No thanks," Louie said. "One race was enough for me."

"Don't think you can do it?" Pete goaded.

Louie didn't answer. He knew it was a trap. Whatever he said Pete would use to prod him further. Louie knew there was no way he was giving up his Saturday-night drinking with the gang.

But Pete would not give up. "You're on the team now, Louie. You're not a quitter, are you?"

Louie rolled his eyes. "How does running one race put me on the team? I came in last, remember?"

"You'll get better. I'll help you."

Louie finally gave in. "Okay. I'll run next week against Banning. If I come in last again, that's the end of it, okay?"

"It's a deal," Pete said. "I know you can do it."

A week later Louie lined up for his second 660-yard race. He was relieved that this would be his last race ever. He didn't plan to deliberately come in last, but he knew he would. The three Banning High School runners were bigger than he was, and they took the whole event seriously. One stretched, and Louie overheard another giving himself a pep talk. It was all too weird. Louie just wanted it over.

At the crack of the starting gun, the Banning runners shot off the starting line. Before long Louie was staring at their backs as he jogged along in last place. Then from the sidelines he heard a group of ninth graders yelling, "Come on, Louie! Come on, Louie!"

Louie was startled. No one had ever cheered for him before. It felt good. He ran faster, passing one runner. Two Banning runners came in first and second, but Louie was third, not last. He was astonished.

"You can do it," Pete said. "Coach says you don't have good form yet, but you have guts, and guts count. Stay on the team. I'll coach you. I think you can go somewhere with this."

"It hurts too much," Louie grumbled, rubbing his calves. "Why would anyone do this to himself?"

"It gets easier. You'll see," Pete said. "Give it a shot. You could be a runner, Louie. I know you could. Remember, a lifetime of glory is worth a moment of pain."

"I don't think so. Track's not for me."

Pete gripped Louie's arm. "Look, the way I see it you have one of two choices. Either keep going the way you're going and be a bum, or put your heart into something worthwhile and see what happens. It's your choice. Tell me tomorrow what you're going to do."

That night Louie hardly slept. He thought about the workers at the Columbia Steel Mill. Their work was dirty and heavy, as was work in the other factories in town or on the oil derricks that surrounded Torrance. Louie thought of his father's hard work to support the family, standing in front of a lathe all day. Was that what he had to look forward to? Louie also thought about the bums who came through town looking for a handout. If he didn't change his ways, would he end up being one of them? Louie wanted something different for himself when he grew up. At the same time, he didn't want to give up his friends and freewheeling life. He didn't know what to do. Would the discipline of training to be a runner really change his life?

By morning Louie had made a decision: he would stay with the track team and let Pete train him, but he wouldn't give up drinking or smoking. He would just drink and smoke secretly.

Almost instantly Louie regretted giving in to Pete. The training sessions Pete devised were torture. Every night after school Pete herded Louie outside to run while he rode alongside on his bike. Whenever Louie slowed down, Pete whacked his bottom with a switch. It worked. Louie ran faster.

More interschool races were held, and Louie never came in last again. He came in second and then first in a 660-yard race. Louie was astonished. He never imagined that hard work could really make that much difference. Louie made the all-city finals, racing against students from high schools throughout the area. He came in fifth place.

At the same track meet, Pete broke the Torrance High School record for the mile. Everyone talked about the Zamperini brothers, Peter and Louis the athletes—not Pete the athlete and his no-good, troublemaking brother Louie. It felt good to Louie, though not good enough to overcome the thought of a long, hot summer working around the house. With no track meets to train for, Louie soon became restless and resentful of all his chores. The train whistles in the distance began to beckon. Louie knew it was only a matter of time before he jumped a train and headed out of town.

Chapter 4

TRAIN WHISTLE BLOW'N

I t was the second Saturday of summer vacation, and Louie had already had enough. "Louis, weed the flowerbed before lunch," his mother said. "Louie, it's your turn to cut the grass," his father reminded him. "Louis, take your sisters to the park." On and on the demands went until Louie blew up and yelled at his father, who yelled back. The two stood eye to eye glaring at each other until Louie finally cursed and headed for his bedroom, where he stuffed some clothes into an old bag and headed out of the house.

"Don't leave, Louie," his mother said through teary eyes. "Please don't leave."

Louie stared at her as if she were a stranger. "I'd be better off anywhere than here," he snapped, and his mother disappeared into the kitchen.

As Louie proceeded out the door, Louise Zamperini ran after her son. As she reached out and hugged Louie, she dropped a wrapped sandwich into his bag. "Come back to us, Louie," she said. "Promise you'll come home."

Louie remained silent and walked down the path.

"Hey, Louie, wait," his father shouted after him.

Louie turned to see his father running down the path.

"Take this," his father said, holding out two one-dollar bills.

Louie hesitated a moment. He had convinced himself that he was a slave around the house, that his parents didn't care. Now he wondered whether that was true. But the gestures weren't enough to change his mind. Louie grabbed the money, turned, and walked away.

His first stop was his friend Johnny's house. Johnny was feeling put upon by his parents too. It was easy for Louie to convince his friend to join him.

The two boys grinned at each other as they stood by the curve in the railroad tracks on the northern edge of town. As the first freight train passed, they slung their bags onto the platform at the back of the caboose and ran alongside. First Johnny pulled himself up onto the train, and then Louie. The boys climbed onto the catwalk on the caboose roof and sat down. It was getting late, and the sun began to set as the train rolled northward. The train stopped in Los Angeles, shunting back and forth to pick up more freight cars before continuing northward. The night was bright and clear, and Louie stared up at the stars and across the moonlit valley toward the San Joaquin River. *This is the way I'm meant to live,* he thought, *free to go wherever I want.*

Louie and Johnny jumped off the train before it reached San Francisco. The sandwich Louise Zamperini had given Louie was now long gone, and the boys were hungry. They walked past an orchard and helped themselves to the early crop of apples and pears. Louie heard thunder in the distance, and soon it began to rain.

By now the boys were on the outskirts of the city, in a hobo camp where hundreds of men, women, and children lived in cardboard and canvas huts. The residents of the camp were thin, and the children stared blankly. Louie looked away as he thought of his two sisters and how happy and lively they were. Louie spotted a man standing with his back to him and Johnny. In the bag slung over the man's shoulder Louie could see a large can of Heinz baked beans. Louie wanted the beans. He nodded at Johnny. The two had been partners in crime many times before. With a second nod, Louie ran up behind the man and grabbed the can of beans from his bag. Johnny was right on his heels. The two took off running.

"Hey, thief," Louie heard the man yell. He laughed as he turned to see three men give chase. There was no way the men would catch the two boys. They didn't, and before long, the three men gave up.

After running a safe distance, Louie and Johnny sat down by the railroad tracks. Johnny used his pocketknife to pry open the can. The two then took turns eating the beans from the can with a stick. Even though Louie wouldn't admit it, the hobo camp had shaken him up. Sitting by the railroad tracks, shivering in the rain, and eating cold baked beans, he began to wonder if he'd been a fool. Just then a passenger train rolled by, and Louie looked up. The train seemed to move in slow motion as it rumbled by. Louie peered into the first-class dining car. He could almost smell the roast beef being served on china plates set on white tablecloths. He could see women in shimmering dresses and men in tuxedos drinking from crystal glasses.

Louie spoke before he thought. "Boy, are we dopes."

Johnny looked at Louie as he poked around in the bottom of the can for the last few beans.

"Yes, sir, we are," Louie said. "One day I'm going to be like them. I'm going to ride in style and eat in a dining car like that. I'm going to order the works, anything I want."

"Yeah, sure," Johnny smirked.

Louie bit his lip. There was something in the contrast between the hobo camp and the first-class dining car that reminded him of what his brother had said to him: "You have one of two choices. Either keep going the way you're going and be a bum, or put your heart into something worthwhile and see what happens. It's your choice."

Did Louie really want to be hungry and homeless like the men at the hobo camp? Was that the life he wanted? He didn't think so.

"Let's go home," Louie said, standing up. He didn't trust himself to say any more. He didn't want Johnny thinking he'd become soft.

The boys were four hundred miles from Torrance, with virtually no money between them. Louie assumed it would be as easy to get back home as it had been to leave. He was wrong.

Louie and Johnny jumped a train headed south and were soon hunched up, tired and wet, in a boxcar with two other bums. Exhausted, the boys drifted off to sleep. Louie awoke suddenly to find the two bums closing in on him and Johnny.

"We want your money," one of the men said.

Louie shook his head and elbowed Johnny awake just as the men pounced. Louie and Johnny sprang to their feet and fought with all their might, beating back their attackers. Bloodied and breathless, the two bums slumped to the floor. But Louie and Johnny weren't done. They dragged the two men to the boxcar door and pushed them from the moving train. With a smile Louie declared that the two bums would have enough bruises to remind them not to mess with him and Johnny again if their paths ever crossed.

Following the fight the two boys went back to sleep. When they awoke, they discovered the boxcar was motionless and the door locked. They were trapped inside! Louie guessed the boxcar had been left on a siding. For three days the two boys remained trapped inside the boxcar, which felt like an oven as it baked in the hot California sun. They were hungry and thirsty, and Louie began to worry they would die if they didn't escape.

Louie came up with a plan. In the boxcar roof was a vent, which Louie pried open while standing on Johnny's shoulders. The opening was narrow, but Louie managed to pull himself up and crawl out onto the roof, slicing his knee open as he did so. After helping Johnny onto the boxcar roof, Louie tied a handkerchief around his knee as tightly as possible to stop the bleeding. After climbing down from the boxcar, the boys stood by the railroad siding. Louie looked at himself. He was dirty, bloodied, and bruised. It strengthened his resolve that being a bum and jumping trains was no ticket to freedom.

The boys jumped another train and made it back to Torrance. As Louie walked up the path to the Zamperinis' clapboard house, the place had never looked so inviting.

Louie's mother rushed out the door, wiping her hands on her apron. "Louie, you're back! My Toots, you came home," she exclaimed, enveloping him in a hug before pulling him inside. "Sit down. Let me see. You're hurt."

"It's nothing, Ma," Louie said.

His mother took no heed as she untied the bloody handkerchief from his knee and tended to the wound, cleaning it, slathering it with ointment, and putting a clean bandage on it. She then took Louie to the kitchen and fed him a pile of cookies. For once Louie didn't feel angry with her. It was nice to have someone care about him.

By the time his father came home from work, Louie had bathed, changed clothes, and started painting the house. From the look on his father's face, Louie knew that his father was glad and surprised, glad his son was safely home and surprised to see him painting the house.

That night Louie slept in his own bed in the room he shared with Pete. After the light was turned off, he said quietly, "Okay, Pete, I give up. I've been a fool. Make me the best runner I can be."

The next morning Louie was ready to train. Once again, while Louie ran, Pete followed on the bicycle, whacking Louie with a switch whenever he slowed down. Despite the whacks, Louie had to stop every two or three blocks to catch his breath. Right there and then he decided to give up smoking and cut down on his drinking. He couldn't let those bad habits hold him back.

That night Pete left a comic book about Glenn Cunningham on Louie's pillow. Louie read it in one sitting. When he finished the comic book, he stared out the window and thought about Glenn Cunningham's life. Glenn was eight years older than Louie and at the time held the record for running the fastest outdoor mile in the United States, but that wasn't the real story. The real story was that when Glenn was seven years old, he and his thirteen-year-old brother Floyd were lighting the wood stove in their one-room schoolhouse when the stove exploded, badly burning both boys. Their older sister called the doctor, and the news was bad. The doctor was sure that Floyd would die a long, slow death and that Glenn would most likely follow the same path.

Floyd did die nine days later from his injuries, but Glenn clung to life. He suffered through infections and pain, but eventually he was able to sit up, and then stand. His leg muscles were deeply burned, and stretching the scar tissue was excruciating. Two years passed before Glenn could walk again. But Glenn would not give up. He discovered it was easier to run than walk, and he often took off running across a field holding onto a mule's tail for balance. Eventually Glenn was well enough to return to school. He also kept running and then winning races. The rest was history.

The next morning, as he trained with Pete, Louie was still thinking about Glenn Cunningham's determination. After the training session, he went straight home and did chores for his mother before taking another run after lunch.

Day after day Louie felt himself getting stronger and faster. By the end of his second week of training, he had made himself run the four miles from his house to Redondo Beach, where he turned around and hitched a ride back to Torrance. By the end of the month, Louie could run both ways, as well as do a two-mile loop along the beach. He discovered that he loved to run outside in nature, and he often spent afternoons in the hills around Torrance running along mountain tracks, hurdling tree stumps and avoiding rattlesnakes. As he ran, his legs grew stronger and his pace became steadier.

Louie wondered how he would do when he went back to school. Pete would no longer be attending Torrance High School. He had graduated and would be attending Compton Junior College, eight miles away, where tuition was free. Louie wondered if he would be able to follow his brother and become the fastest runner at Torrance High School.

"You can do that and so much more!" Pete urged him.

Louie wasn't so sure.

Chapter 5

TORRANCE TORNADO

I n fall 1932, following summer vacation, Louie returned to school. He felt like he'd been deposited on an alien planet. He worked hard at his studies and continued to excel on the track. Before long, the kids who had taunted him in elementary and junior high welcomed him into their cliques. Louie was invited to ukulele cookouts at the beach and to other parties, and on his sixteenth birthday, January 26, 1933, the girls in his class chased him down the corridor and gave him sixteen birthday spankings, giggling and cracking jokes at the same time. Louie couldn't have been happier with his "punishment."

Louie could barely believe how things had changed. He had to admit that Pete was right: changing your attitude also changed a lot of other things. Whenever he ran into Johnny or other members of his old gang, he found it hard to understand how he had ever thought they were living the good life. It seemed such a futile existence now.

Although Pete had a dorm room at Compton Junior College, he drove his old Chevy home nearly every night to supervise Louie's running. He put so much effort into Louie's training that it made Louie take the matter seriously. Louie soon made a pact with himself, one that he didn't even tell Pete about. Louie would train every day for a year, regardless of the weather. On the days when it rained and he couldn't train on the muddy track at school, he pulled on his shorts and tennis shoes and took a one-and-a-half-mile run around his neighborhood. On two occasions sand storms swept over Torrance, but Louie stuck to his pact, tying a handkerchief over his mouth to avoid breathing in the sand as he ran.

The Zamperini family all got behind Louie's efforts. When Louie complained that the high school's woolen athletic shorts itched, his mother made him a pair of lightweight shorts from her black, pleated satin skirt. And every Saturday that Louie had a track meet, Pete was there too. The two brothers developed a system. As a race approached, Louie would stretch and limber up and then lie face-down on the infield grass and imagine the race. When the race was about to begin, he would take his place on the starting line and burst forward at the sound of the starting gun. As Louie ran, Pete, in the infield, would sprint back and forth with a stopwatch yelling instructions and encouragement to his brother.

Louie's speed was astonishing. He won an 880-yard race and in the process broke the school record, held by Pete, by two seconds. The more Louie ran, the faster he got. He ran a cross-country mile in 5 minutes, 3 seconds (5:03), and then he ran the same distance in 4:58.

In November 1933, near the end of his sophomore year, Louie entered a two-mile practice run with Pete. The two brothers lined up against thirteen other runners at Compton Junior College. Louie was one of two runners still in high school. The other was fellow Torrance High runner La Verne Jones. Louie started fast and got faster. Before he knew it, he was bursting through the finish tape. He turned to see that the next competitor was still fifty yards behind, while Pete was in third place. Louie's victory led to a story about him in the *Torrance Herald*, the local newspaper. The article ended with the following words:

The boys [Louie and La Verne Jones] went into the practice run without any preliminary training, merely for the experience, and young Zamperini surprised even himself by taking first place easily. The showing of the Torrance boys was all the more remarkable since they were competing way over their heads against older and more experienced runners representing junior colleges.

Following the two-mile race at Compton, Louie kept improving. He could consistently run a mile in 4:28 or 4:29. Everyone at Torrance High knew him by name, and in February 1934, the start of his junior year, Louie was elected junior class president. Despite the fame, Louie struggled to keep up his grades. And while he sometimes became frustrated with various subjects, he knew he had to keep at them if he wanted to get into college and keep running.

Torrance High School belonged to the Marine Athletic League, and in May 1934 Louie entered the Marine League three-quarter-mile race. The *Torrance Herald* recorded the result in the May 18 edition. The headline read, "Zamperini Sets New Record." The article that followed said:

For the first time in years, if ever, Torrance high school colors were out in front in the finals of the big Southern California meet, held at Los Angeles high school field Saturday. Louis Zamperini, crack miler for the Red and White, who has led the field in every race he has entered this year, turned the trick with a sensational victory in the Class B distance event, 1320 yards, when he set a new record for the event of 3:17. This tops by more than three seconds the old mark which has stood for several seasons.

Louie was astonished at how far he had come. Less than a year ago he had run away from home to be a hobo, and now he was a star athlete at school. Louie's mother bought a scrapbook and cut out the article from the *Torrance Herald*. "You're just beginning, Toots," she told him. She appeared to be right. Louie had not lost a race he had entered all year, and he continued to keep his personal pledge of running every day.

By now Louie had his sights on the large interschool track meet coming up at the Los Angeles Coliseum, where he was entered in the mile race. Louie knew he would have some tough competition. The best miler in the district, Virgil Hooper from Antelope Valley, was the favorite to win. He'd been officially timed at 4:24 for the mile and held the state high school record for the distance at 4:29.2. Three other boys in the race also offered stiff competition: Bob Jordan from Whittier High, and two Native Americans, Elmo Lomachutzkeoma and Abbot Lewis, from the Sherman Institute.

Louie went over the race a million times in his mind, discussing endless strategies with Pete. Pete said the only person Louie had to worry about was Virgil Hooper. If Louie was to beat him, he needed to run a smart race. If after 220 yards Louie was ahead of Virgil, he was to run even faster and try to open as big a lead as he could. Pete pointed out that when Louie reached the final 220 yards of the race, if he had a lead of ten to fifteen yards on Virgil and ran the final distance in 30 seconds, Virgil would have to run that distance in about 27 seconds to make up the distance on Louie. At that stage of the race, it would be hard to do. Louie took in everything his brother said.

On the morning of the track meet, Louie felt terrible. His stomach was tied in knots, and he couldn't eat any breakfast.

Pete eyed him suspiciously. "What's the matter, Toots? You scared?" he asked.

Louie's temper flared. "No, I just don't feel good. I don't expect you to understand!"

"The heck I don't," Pete said.

"I said I don't feel good, that's all," Louie yelled, slamming his hand down on the table.

"Aw, you're just chicken," Pete yelled back.

Louie felt his face turn red with anger. How dare his brother call him chicken after all they'd gone through! He turned to his mother and blurted, "I'm going onto that track, and I'm going to run. If I drop dead on the track, my legs will still keep running!"

His mother nodded and filled his coffee cup.

Pete was grinning. "That's the stuff," he said.

Louie felt better, but his nervous stomach returned at the Coliseum in Los Angeles, where the 1932 Olympic Games had been held. When he walked to the starting line for the mile race, he was astounded to discover that so many runners were entered they had to line up in two rows, one behind the other. Louie drew the second row. As the starter's pistol cracked, he seethed about his poor starting position. Even though the race had started, Louie had to wait for runners in front before he could even move. Once he started running, so many runners were on the track that Louie couldn't find an open lane to run in. Meanwhile, Elmo and Abbot were out in front and setting a blistering pace.

In the second lap Louie found some space to pass other runners and move up in the race. In the third lap a number of the runners tired and dropped back, but not Louie. He kept a steady pace. A little over halfway through the race, Elmo and Abbot also began to tire, and Louie passed them. Virgil Hooper was still in the race but suffering from a carbuncle on the back of his neck. He eventually dropped out. With two hundred yards to go, Louie had the lead.

Pete sprinted along on the infield grass urging Louie not to slow but to keep his pace. Suddenly Louie felt the foot of another runner tap his heal. It was Gaylord Mercer from Glendale High, and he was gaining on Louie. Louie bolted into a sprint, crossing the finish line ten yards ahead of Gaylord.

From his disadvantaged start position, Louie had come from behind to win the race. He not only won but also broke the world record for the Interscholastic Mile, a record that had stood for eighteen years. The old record was 4:23.6. Louie ran the race in 4:21.3.

Back in Torrance, news of Louie's track successes had always appeared in the sports section on page four of the *Torrance Herald*. This time the story of his record-breaking win was on the front page. The headline read, "18 YEAR OLD RECORD FALLS BEFORE FLYING ZAMPERINI." Beneath the headline was a photo of Louie, arms outstretched as he crossed the finish line, with no other runners in sight. The accompanying article declared,

> Hail the World's Champion. Torrance fans in the stands at the Coliseum went wild with enthusiasm last Saturday afternoon when they watched Louis Zamperini swing around the oval four times to finish yards ahead of the fastest field ever assembled in the mile in the Southern California finals and set the remarkable record of 4 minutes 21.3 seconds for the event.

Louie had run the fastest mile ever recorded by a high school student. He found it hard to believe how far he had come. Now in his junior year of high school, Louis Zamperini, the "Wop" kid headed in the wrong direction, was now being written about in every newspaper in the state. The newspapers had a nickname for him, the "Torrance Tornado."

Louie laughed when he learned the *Torrance Herald* had insured his legs for $50,000. "What about my arms?" he joked. "I can't run without them, either."

It seemed everyone wanted to see Louie race. When he ran practice laps at school, a crowd gathered outside the chain-link fence, cheering him on. Students and parents carpooled to every track meet he ran in. He was presented with gold watches and bags of groceries, grade-school kids wanted to tag along behind him, and the city fathers lined up to shake his hand.

As Louie entered his final year of high school, college scholarship offers arrived daily in the mail. They made Louie laugh. No one else at Torrance High School, not even the straight-A students, was getting the kind of attention from colleges he was. As graduation neared, Louie had to make an important decision. The year before, Pete had won a scholarship to the University of Southern California (USC) in Los Angeles. At USC he continued running and earned a spot as one of the top ten college milers in the country. Louie knew his success was linked to Pete's dedicated training, and he wanted to stay near him.

Also, eight months and six thousand miles away, the biggest sporting event in the world would be taking place—the 1936 Olympic Games in Berlin, Germany. Louie wondered if he might make it to the games as a runner. He knew it was audacious to think so. Elite runners didn't peak till their late twenties, and he was only eighteen and about to graduate from high school. Louie knew it was a crazy notion, but a letter he kept tucked in his shirt pocket reassured him it might be possible. Louie often took it out and read:

Dear Louis Zamperini,

By your performance you have marked yourself as one of the outstanding candidates for the American Olympics Team. All of the athletes with whom members of the Amer-

ican Olympic committee have talked have favored participation in the 1936 games. It is the duty of the committee to
provide for this participation and to raise funds necessary
to finance the team. Outsiders have challenged the decision
of the committee, claiming that many athletes do not want
to go. To refute this challenge and remove it as an obstacle
to contributions to the fund, the committee desires an ex-
pression from a large number of actual candidates. Are you
planning to try out for the team, and if you qualify, will
you be ready to make the trip to the 1936 Games in Berlin?
Please indicate your intentions on the enclosed card, by an
X marked in the "Yes" or "No" square, and send it by return
mail. Thanks for your co-operation.

> Sincerely yours, Avery Brundage, President,
> American Olympic Committee

Louie had marked a large X in the "yes" square and returned the
card right away. He knew the letter had been necessary because of
the rise of Adolf Hitler and the Nazis in Germany. Some Americans
argued that the Olympics shouldn't be held in Berlin. All Louie knew
was that he wanted a chance to make the team and compete against
the best runners in the world.

Chapter 6

A BRILLIANT RACE

On a cool February morning in 1936, Louie pulled his car to a halt outside the stately Kappa Sigma fraternity house with its red brick facade and white columns. His brother Pete was a member of the fraternity. As he lifted a suitcase from the trunk, Louie was sure he'd made the right decision accepting a scholarship to the University of Southern California. He had also struck a deal with the university: he would stay with Pete in the fraternity house and train with the other students but would not start classes until fall. That way Louie could spend his time focusing on getting into the Olympics.

Louie felt intense pressure. The *Torrance Herald* had urged the town to get behind him:

> All Torrance wants to see Louie on that world famous team. There is only one way to accomplish this and that is by getting behind the boy with all the resources this community has. He will do his part in bringing world renown to this community. Louie's spectacular successes of the past two years are an indication of what he can do this year. "On to Berlin" is his slogan of the hour, and it should be the slogan of Torrance.

While Louie was grateful for the faith the citizens of Torrance placed in him, doubts crept in as he failed to meet some of the milestones Pete had set for him. Louie was lagging behind in his training schedule. He improved his running times every week but not enough to secure a place on the 1,500-meter team going to the Olympics. When the Zamperini brothers learned that Glenn Cunningham had clocked a 4:09 mile, they had a serious talk. Louie was averaging eight seconds slower than Cunningham's time, the equivalent of seventy-five yards behind on the track.

Louie didn't have enough training time left to make up the difference. It was a bitter moment for him. Torrance was watching Louie, cheering him on to be their Olympic representative, but Louie knew he didn't have the edge he needed to make the trials. Finally Pete suggested Louie aim for the 1940 Olympic Games. Louie would be twenty-three years old then, closer to the age of the country's best milers. Louie knew Pete was right. There would be no Olympic Games for him this year. He covered his disappointment by partying with the Kappa Sigma frat boys.

On May 8, while he skimmed through the *Los Angeles Times*, an article about a track event called the Compton Invitational caught Louie's eye. In two weeks' time, Norman Bright, the second fastest 5,000-meter runner in the United States, would be running in Los Angeles.

"Look, Norman Bright's running in the Los Angeles Coliseum in two weeks," Louie told Pete.

"Do you want to go see him?" Pete asked.

Louie wasn't sure. Norman Bright, along with Don Lash, performed so well that he and Don were almost guaranteed two of the three spots in the 5,000-meter division of the US Olympic team.

"Better yet, you should enter, Toots! Go for it. Of course Don Lash will be on the team, but if you can stay up with Bright, the third spot would be yours!"

Louie shook his head. "Pete, that's 5,000 meters you're talking about—three miles and 188 yards. I'm a miler, remember. I run four laps around the track. Now you think I can magically do twelve?"

Pete put his hands on Louie's shoulders. "This is your best shot. I can feel it," he said.

"You really think so?"

"What do you have to lose? I'll get you ready. You're in great shape, but you're not going to make the 1,500 team. Let's give this a try. What do you have going on that's more important than the Olympics?"

This was an interesting question. Louie didn't have much else to do until classes started. "Really? You think we can do this? There's only two weeks to train."

"What are we sitting around for, then?" Pete said with a grin. "Let's make a 5,000-meter runner out of you."

Louie loved the enormous challenge. He trained so hard he wore the skin off his toes, but he didn't stop. He worked tirelessly preparing himself for the race.

Ten thousand spectators were seated in the Coliseum to watch as Louie lined up for the start of the 5,000 meters. Louie's mind ran over the instructions Pete had given him. Norman Bright liked to conserve energy during the race, saving his strength for a final sprint to the finish. Pete told Louie to stick with Norman as closely as possible and at the start of the final lap open into a sprint for the finish line. Stationed on the infield, Pete would tell Louie when he was on the final lap.

At the crack of the starting gun, Louie took off, Norman Bright beside him. Other runners in the race began to fall back, leaving Louie and Norman out in front. The two matched each other as they ran. When Pete yelled it was the final lap, Louie bolted into a sprint, passing Norman. However, Pete had miscounted, and it was actually the second-to-last lap. Norman passed Louie as the crowd cheered. Then Louie passed Norman. Back and forth the two runners went, each taking the lead from the other. Norman ran on the inside lane, with Louie on his outside. Louie could tell that his competitor was tiring. He sprinted harder and took the lead as they headed for the final stretch. As the two runners were about to lap a competitor, race officials motioned for the runner to yield the way and move to the right. As he did so, he ran right in front of Louie. Trying to avoid a collision, Louie moved to the far right lane, but the runner kept moving right. Louie took a side step to pass him on the inside but lost his balance and had to put a hand down on the track for a moment. Once he'd steadied himself, he headed for the inside lane. Norman was well ahead, and Louie put every ounce of his strength into sprinting to catch him. The crowd went wild as Louie gained on Norman, catching him at the finish line. Norman crossed the line just two inches in front of Louie.

Louie was elated. Both he and Norman Bright had run the fastest 5,000-meter race recorded in the United States so far that year, a feat that would earn both runners a trip to the upcoming Olympic trials. Louie could hardly believe his performance. It seemed like a dream. He had managed to keep up with Norman throughout the race and would soon be on his way across the country to Randall's Island in New York City, where the Olympic trials were being held.

Louie worried about going to the trials alone. Pete had been his constant companion and coach. How would he do without him? It would cost too much time and money for Pete to go with him to New York, but that didn't stop Louie from begging Pete to go along. Pete always gave the same reply: "It's time you went out on your own. You'll be fine. I'll be listening on the radio—I bet the whole of Torrance will be too."

Torrance did rally around Louie. Shop owners donated clothes and toiletries, citizens gave money, and the Southern Pacific Railroad Company presented him with a free pass to travel anywhere within the United States for a year. Louie even received a suitcase from the Torrance Chamber of Commerce. He cringed when he read the words "Louis Zamperini, The Torrance Tornado, Torrance, Calif." stenciled in large letters on top. Louie knew he would be teased about that.

On Friday, July 3, 1936, a large group of Torrance citizens accompanied Louie to the railroad station in Los Angeles. Many other athletes from the West Coast were gathered to catch the train. With a lot of cheering, confetti, and backslapping, Louie boarded the train. He gave a final wave to his parents and Pete and settled into his seat. He was on his way from the West Coast to the East Coast on a train—with a ticket! It was a novel feeling. Louie thought of the time four years before when he and Johnny ran away and jumped a freight train north. He remembered how outside San Francisco in the rain he was looking at people sitting in the dining car of a passing train and how he had said to Johnny, "One day I'm going to be like them. I'm going to ride in style and eat in a dining car like that. I'm going to order the works, anything I want." Louie was now riding on a train with a dining car where he could order the works. It felt good. He'd come a long way in the intervening years, but he still had a long way to go to get to participate in the Berlin Olympics.

The trip across the country took four days, with an extended stop in Chicago so that the athletes could work out at the University of Chicago's Stagg Field. Chicago was hot—unbelievably hot, with the temperature reaching 100 degrees Fahrenheit. Louie had read about the heat wave engulfing much of the United States. It was the worst heat wave the country had experienced since meteorological records had begun being kept in 1895.

Louie had been right about the suitcase: everyone made fun of it. It became a ritual for one of the athletes to hold it out the window when they entered a station and yell, "Look, we have the Torrance Tornado on board."

By the time the train arrived at Penn Station in New York City, the temperature was 106 degrees. A headline in the *New York Times* announced that twelve people had died from heatstroke in the city the day before.

From the station, Louie made his way twelve blocks up Eighth Avenue to Hotel Lincoln, where he and Norman would split the cost of a room. Once the United States Olympic team was chosen, the US Olympic committee would pay for the accommodation, travel, and food of the selected athletes. Until then, each athlete covered his or her own expenses. Louie was grateful for the free train ticket and money the businessmen of Torrance had collected on his behalf. He hoped that sharing a room with Norman in the 27-story, 1,331-room hotel, the largest in the city, would help keep his expenses as low as possible.

Norman had arrived in New York City a few days earlier to run in a 10,000-meter race. He told Louie it was too hot to run outside, but what choice did they have, with the Olympic trials just a few days away? Louie agreed. He'd been sweating profusely by the time he reached the hotel, and that was after a slow walk up the street. Norman told him that the track was so hot the spikes on his running shoes burned the bottoms of his feet, which were now battered and blistered.

The hotel room was small, with a window above the doorway. The air inside was stifling, and Louie began to wonder how he would fare competing outdoors in such heat. He was sure it was a thought every athlete arriving in New York for the Olympic trials was pondering.

Once settled into the room, Louie sat on the bed and scanned the sports section of the *New York Times.* He read the sports writers' predictions of how the runners would finish in the 5,000 meters, which would be run on Sunday, July 12. Louie soon realized he wasn't even mentioned! The writer was focused on East Coast runners. Louie was indignant. He wrote to Pete, "In the papers out here they have picked the place of winners for Sunday's 5000 meters: (1) Lash, (2) Bright, (3) Lochner, (4) Ottey, (5) Deckard—and they don't even know I'm out here. . . . If I have my strength left from this heat, I'll beat Bright and give Lash the scare of his life and then I'll make the print."

Louie hardly slept that night. His bed was narrow, the room was too hot, and the sounds of the city outside never stopped. Despite his lack of sleep, Louie was up early the next morning to train. But even early in the morning it was so hot that Louie could barely drink enough fluids to prevent dehydration. And despite eating as much as he could, his weight dropped under the strain of training in such conditions. Louie's five-foot-eleven frame weighed 140 pounds when he boarded the train in Los Angeles. After three days in New York City, he was down to 132 pounds and dropping.

Louie's only consolation was that all the runners—he and his competitors—were struggling with the conditions. One athlete bought round-the-clock tickets to the movies so that he could doze off in the back seat of one of the few air-conditioned buildings in the city. Louie didn't have the money for round-the-clock tickets, but whenever he could, he would sit through a movie just to get out of the heat.

Five days after arriving in New York, it was time for Louie to see what he was made of. The Olympic trials had begun the day before, with the official opening of Randall's Island Stadium, built for the event. The day of the 5,000-meter race was another scorcher. Louie and Norman left the hotel together and took a bus to the East River and then a boat upriver to Randall's Island. Despite the fierce heat, thousands of spectators were seated at the stadium to watch the day's activities.

Louie breathed deeply and tried to relax awaiting the start of the 5,000-meter race. Twelve men were in the race, and Louie was sure that if Pete were there, he would tell him to conserve his energy for the end, slip into the inside lane behind the lead runners, and stay close enough to them to make his move when the time came. Louie also reassured himself that he didn't have to beat Don Lash, the race favorite. If he finished in second or third place, he would make the US Olympic team.

At the start of the 5,000-meter race, Louie took his place at the starting line. Once the race began, he maneuvered himself into the position he'd planned. Don Lash took the lead, with Norman Bright giving chase. Several other runners, including Tom Deckard, were also ahead.

The track felt like an inferno beneath Louie's feet, but Louie kept moving. The heat, though, was having an effect on other runners in the race. A runner in front collapsed from heat exhaustion, and Louie hurdled over him. Then the heat began taking a toll on Norman Bright, who took a sideways step off the track and twisted his ankle before getting his balance. Louie pulled alongside his roommate and encouraged him to go on, but Norman was spent. "Louie, I can't do it," he said. "Make your move. Go on without me."

Louie entered the final lap in third place. He was gaining on Don

Lash, who ran just behind Tom Deckard. For a moment Louie lost concentration and failed to make his move on the leader when he should have. Entering the final turn, he realized it was now or never. Just then Don passed Tom, forcing Louie to move to the third lane to pass Tom himself and causing him to lose precious ground. Louie quickly moved back to the second lane and poured every ounce of his strength into a sprint for the finish line. Louie and Don crossed the finish line side by side.

Louie breathed deeply waiting for the official results. Since he was gaining on Don at the finish line, he thought he'd won the race. When the announcer gave the results, Don had won, with Louie in second place. Norman had kept running and finished fifth. A third of the runners who started the race failed to finish, most of them collapsing from the heat.

A little dejected by the result, Louie headed to the locker room. Moments later an official rushed in and led him back to the track, where he was handed a certificate that read "First Place." Louie was confused. The official explained that after film of the race finish had been reviewed, the race had been declared a dead heat. Louie and Don had both finished first. A feeling of joy rushed through Louie when he realized that not only had he tied Don Lash, the American record holder for the distance, but also he had secured his place on the US Olympic team. In just three days he would be headed for Berlin to participate in the Eleventh Olympiad!

The remainder of the day was a whirlwind. At nineteen years of age, Louie was still registered as being from Torrance High School and had gone from Olympic hopeful to hero in just one race. Sixteen telegrams awaited him at the hotel. That night a New York businessman took him to dinner. When he got back to his room, Louie couldn't help including the experience in an open letter to the

Torrance Herald: "I ate in a skyscraper dining room where it cost two of us, the fellow who took me and I [*sic*], $7.00. Boy, what a snazzy place."

The three days flew by. Louie met with the Olympic committee members and the other athletes who made the team. Among them were men Louie had followed since starting running in high school. He felt like pinching himself as he sat opposite his all-time hero Glenn Cunningham as they filled out paperwork for their German visas. It was a thrill to stand in the uniform-fitting line beside Jesse Owens and Frank Wykoff, who'd won gold medals in the 4 x 100-meter relay in the previous two Olympics.

The uniforms were an issue. Everyone had lost weight competing during the heat wave. Louie tipped the scales at 125 pounds, 15 pounds lighter than when he had started out from Los Angeles. The white pants and navy blue blazer with the Olympic shield on each button hung loosely on him. Louie hoped to gain some weight on the nine-day voyage across the Atlantic to Hamburg, Germany.

At noon on Wednesday, July 15, 1936, the SS *Manhattan* was due to sail for Germany with all 334 members of the US Olympic team aboard. Before heading to the ship, Louie taped over the words "Torrance Tornado" on his suitcase. He didn't want to spend the voyage being teased by his Olympic companions.

As Louie climbed the gangplank to board the ship at Pier 60 on the Hudson River, a brass band played on the dock, newspaper photographers flashed pictures, and movie cameramen filmed footage for newsreels. Thousands of New Yorkers stood around the dock waving American flags. Since it was the first time Louie had sailed on an ocean liner, he had to admit the SS *Manhattan* was an impressive vessel. The ship was 668 feet long and weighed 24,289 tons. Her black hull and white superstructure gleamed in the sunlight, and her twin red funnels were trimmed at the top by white and blue stripes. Red, white, and blue bunting was everywhere on the ship and dock. As he boarded the vessel, Louie was presented with a small American flag to wave from the deck at departure.

After stowing his luggage, Louie gathered with the other Olympians on deck. It was midday. He peered over the rail as the crowd below chanted, "Ray! Ray! Ray! For the USA!" The band played the national anthem, and the bow and stern lines were let go. Tugboats began pulling the ship from the dock into the main current of the river. Louie waved until the chanting of the crowd faded.

The SS *Manhattan* began making her way down the Hudson River. Sailing down the west side of Manhattan Island, with the Statue of Liberty passing to starboard, Louie was thankful for the cooling breeze wafting across the deck. As the ship left New York behind, Louie wondered what lay ahead and how he'd perform as a member of the US Olympic team.

Chapter 7

THE BOY WITH
THE FAST FINISH

L ying on his bunk the first night at sea, listening to the throb of the engines and the slap of the ocean against the ship, Louie marveled that he'd made the team. All the hard work and sacrifice had been worth it. He, Louis Silvie Zamperini, was on his way to Berlin to compete in the Olympic Games.

The next morning he scoped out the ship. Many of the Olympic officials were housed in first-class cabins on the upper decks, where the athletes were allowed only if they were training on the promenade deck that wrapped around the vessel. That was where Louie would train, dodging deckchairs and passengers as he went. Athletes would be training in almost every outside space onboard. For some sports, training on a ship was difficult. It was almost impossible for the gymnasts to stay on the balance beam as the SS *Manhattan* rolled from side to side in the swell. And the wind kept blowing ball after ball overboard as the basketball team practiced shooting baskets on the sundeck. Louie laughed aloud when he saw the water polo team training in the pool. The ship's constant motion caused large waves to form on the pool surface. The men on the water polo team looked like they were trying to body surf.

Louie settled into a routine of running laps on the promenade deck in the morning, and then eating—lots of eating. The food

choices on the ship were overwhelming. Each meal was like a ban-
quet, and since the food was free, Louie couldn't resist. One day he
ate the biggest lunch of his life, noting on a napkin that he had consumed one pint of pineapple juice, two bowls of soup, four rolls,
four pickles, two helpings of chicken and sweet potatoes, three dishes
of ice cream and cookies, an apple, a plate of cherries, an orange, and
three pieces of angel food cake. Louie found the pounds he'd lost
from training and running in the heat quickly returning.

The members of the Olympic team practiced, ate, and partied
their way across the Atlantic. The ship stopped at Le Havre on the
north coast of France to load and unload cargo, and Louie got his
first glimpse of Continental Europe. The athletes stayed aboard
during the stop. Louie contented himself by peering over the side
of the ship at men wearing berets and women riding by on bicy-
cles waving. He wondered what it had been like for his grandparents
and his father, who had crossed the Atlantic in the other direction,
landing in the United States, their heads filled with dreams of a better life. Now he was back in Europe with the dream of winning an
Olympic medal for the country his family had adopted.

Around dinnertime on July 23 the SS *Manhattan* reached the
mouth of the Elbe River. As the ship made its way upriver to Hamburg, Louie stood on deck and watched as the German countryside
passed on either side of the ship. Throngs of Germans lined the
shores, waving and cheering as the ship slid by in the moonlight.

At ten o'clock the next morning, Louie was dressed in his formal
US Olympic team uniform—white pants and shirt, navy blazer, and
white straw hat, called a boater. It was time to go ashore. An enthusiastic crowd mobbed the team as they disembarked. On the dock
oompah bands played, and little girls in smocks ran up to the athletes with bunches of flowers. Louie waved as he climbed onto a bus

on the way to the team's first official reception. Several other receptions were held before everyone was herded onto a train for Berlin.

As the team rolled along, Louie thought about the giant red swastika painted on the black train. He'd never been interested in social studies at school. Even so, a chill went down his spine. He was now in Hitler's Germany, and the world was in the grip of some ominous changes. In March, Hitler had moved troops into the Rhineland, remilitarizing the area, a violation of the Treaty of Versailles, the peace settlement signed after the Great War ended in 1918. Then in May, after six months of fighting, Italian troops had overrun Ethiopia. And just two weeks before, a nasty civil war had erupted in Spain.

When the train pulled into the station in Berlin, there were more oompah bands, more crowds, and more cheering. The American team was transferred to open-top buses and driven down Unter den Linden, passing through the Brandenburg Gate and on past Charlottenburg Palace. From his perch on the bus, Louie could see it all. Not a thing seemed to be out of place, and not a scrap of garbage could be seen anywhere. Every building in Berlin was draped in huge red-and-black swastika flags. Germans lined the streets, singing, waving, and cheering as the buses passed.

When the team arrived at the new Olympic Village in Charlottenburg, Louie was captivated by the accommodations. Beech forest and picturesque lakes surrounded the athletes' cottages and gave the setting a fairy-tale feel. It seemed even more fairy-tale like when Louie learned that one of his roommates was Jesse Owens, who would be competing in the 100-meter and 200-meter sprints, the 4 x 100-meter relay, and the long jump. Jesse was considered a gold-medal contender in each event. Louie wished Pete were there to share the experience.

The Olympic Games were to officially open in one week, and Louie used the time to train hard and take stock of his competition in the 5,000 meters. Everyone agreed the Finns were the team to beat. Finnish runners had won the 5,000-meter gold medal in the previous three Olympics. The Finnish runners this time around were Lauri Lehtinen, who had won gold at the 1932 Los Angeles Olympics, Gunnar Höckert, and Ilmari Salminen. They were all older and more experienced than Louie. Even though he knew it would be hard to beat these three in the race, Louie was determined to give it his best shot.

On Saturday, August 1, 1936, the athletes were driven to the opening ceremony at the Olympic stadium. When he saw the stadium for the first time, Louie was impressed. The place was enormous. It was the largest stadium in the world and could seat 110,000 spectators. The athletes lined up by country on the Maifeld, the expansive lawn outside the stadium, waiting for the opening ceremony to begin. As he waited, Louie watched the *Hindenburg* airship fly majestically over the stadium trailing an Olympic flag behind.

At 3:45 Adolf Hitler arrived and made his way to his viewing booth inside. An orchestra played the German national anthem, and the Olympic teams—led, as tradition dictated, by the Greek team—began marching in, eight abreast. Louie waited patiently as the teams entered the stadium in alphabetical order. When it was the US team's turn, Louie adjusted his boater, held his head high, and followed the stars-and-stripes flag.

Louie was stunned by the sight inside. He'd never seen so many people together in one place. The crowd cheered and applauded the American team. When the team marched past Hitler, the leader of the host country, they were supposed to give the Olympic salute, holding the right arm out straight at shoulder height with the palm of the hand down. But since this closely resembled the Nazi salute, the American team had decided ahead of time not to do this. Instead, Louie and the other members of the team slid off their boaters and held them over their hearts as the cheering faded away.

When all the teams had taken their place on the infield, Hitler stepped to the microphone and declared the Eleventh Olympic Games officially open. Twenty thousand doves were released, and a volley of cannon fire boomed outside the stadium. A lone runner holding a burning torch entered the stadium through the eastern gate. He ran around the track and up the stairs at the western end to a large metal bowl. He touched the torch to the bowl, which burst into flame. The crowd went wild. The opening ceremony was over. Louie had never before experienced anything like it. He would never find the right words to describe it to his family back home in Torrance.

Later that evening it was announced that the 1940 Olympic Games would be held in Tokyo. Louie smiled at the news. At the Olympic Village, the Japanese team had emerged the favorite, partly because of their eagerness to give gifts to almost everyone they came into contact with. Louie wondered how much more generous they might be when the games were held in their own country. He promised himself he'd work hard to be there to represent the United States in the distance he preferred—1,500 meters.

Competition began the next day, and Louie took time out to watch his roommate Jesse Owens race in the 100-meter sprint. Jesse won his heats by a wide margin and then won the gold medal in the final race the following day. Louie also watched Glenn Cunningham race the 1,500 meters. Competition in the race was fierce. The first five finishers in the final, including Glenn Cunningham, who finished second, all beat the Olympic record. But it was New Zealander,

Jack Lovelock, who stole the show. Wearing his distinctive black singlet emblazoned with a large silver fern, he streaked to the front, finishing the distance in 3:47.8—a new world record. Louie set his sights on beating that mark in the 1940 Olympics.

On August 4 it was Louie's turn to run. The 5,000 meters had three heats, with the top five finishers advancing to the final three days later. Although Louie wasn't confident he could beat the Finns, he was pretty sure he could make the final. He raced in the third heat, along with Finn Lauri Lehtinen. Louie finished fifth, just scraping into the finals. When he looked at his race time, he was encouraged. Louie's heat was by far the fastest, and his time of 15:02.2 was actually faster than Gunnar Höckert's, winner of the second heat. Don Lash had also made the final with a time of 15:04.4.

The 5,000-meter final was held on Friday, August 7. One hundred thousand spectators, along with Adolf Hitler, were in the stadium to watch the race. Louie was nervous. It was the biggest race of his life.

Following the start, Louie settled into the middle of the field of runners, keeping a steady pace. Don Lash took the early lead, the three Finnish runners right behind. And that was how the race stayed for a number of laps. Louie noticed that Don and the Finns were edging farther ahead of the pack. He wanted to up his pace and not let the frontrunners slip out of reach, but somehow he couldn't manage it. His body felt heavy and slow. He was tiring and couldn't muster his normal speed. He began slipping backward to twelfth place—only three runners were now behind him.

Louie realized that the Finns were too far ahead to catch. They had overtaken Don, who was beginning to fall back in the field. As he ran, Louie thought about something Pete told him several years before. "Remember, a lifetime of glory is worth a moment of pain." Pete was right. Louie was competing in a final at the Olympic Games. How did he want people to remember him?

Entering the second-to-last lap, Louie knew it was time for a moment of pain. As he forced his legs to pump faster and gathered speed, he began passing other runners as he made up ground. Entering the final lap, Louie made himself go even faster. When he rounded the final bend, he was running at a full sprint. As he approached the finish line, he thought he might pass Italian runner Umberto Cerati, but he couldn't. He finished in eighth place. Gunnar Höckert and Lauri Lehtinen came first and second, with Swedish runner Henry Jonsson in third place. Ilmari Salminen, the other Finnish runner, tripped during the race and finished sixth, while Don Lash placed thirteenth. Louie's final time for the race was 14:46.8, the fastest an American runner had run 5,000 meters in 1936. When Louie looked over his individual lap times, he was astounded by how fast he'd run the final lap—56 seconds. Anything under 70 seconds for the last lap was considered fast. In fact, no one had ever before run the last lap of an Olympic 5,000-meter race in that time. Louie was elated. Pete had been right: a few moments of pain had been so worth it.

Following the race Louie showered, changed his clothes, and climbed into the stadium to sit with several other American athletes to watch the final of the men's 110-meter hurdles. The athletes found a spot to sit near the viewing box built for Adolf Hitler and his entourage. As they sat waiting for the hurdles to start, one of the other athletes pointed to the pale, thin man with the long, drawn face sitting near Hitler and said, "That's Joseph Goebbels, the minister of propaganda." Louie nodded, though he wasn't sure what a minister of propaganda did. But Louie wanted a photo of the German chancellor, and since Goebbels was sitting close by, Louie went over and asked him to take his camera and snap a picture of Adolf Hitler.

"What is your name, and what event were you in?" Goebbels asked.

"I'm Louis Zamperini. I just ran in the 5,000-meter final," Louie said.

Goebbels nodded, took Louie's camera, and snapped a photo of the chancellor. Louie noticed him whisper in Hitler's ear. When he returned the camera, Goebbels said, "The führer has asked to see you."

Moments later Louie found himself standing in the space directly below Adolf Hitler's viewing box. Dressed in an immaculately pressed uniform, the führer leaned over and reached for Louie. Louie reached up, and they touched hands. Then Hitler said to him, "*Ah, sie sind der Junge mit dem schnellen Endspurt.*" An interpreter turned to Louie and said, "Our führer says, 'Ah, you are the boy with the fast finish.'"

Louie smiled. It was a good description to take home.

The next day, his Olympic racing over, Louie decided to venture into Berlin. He was eager to try some of the German beer he'd heard so much about. He and another American athlete dressed in their Olympic uniforms and took a bus into the city center, where they found a quiet cafe in which to relax.

Afterward, Louie decided it was time to find a good souvenir to take home with him. The two athletes were walking down Wilhelmstrasse when they noticed a black Mercedes pull up to the building across the street. Adolf Hitler stepped out of the car and walked inside. As he watched Hitler, Louie noticed the small Nazi flag above the door. He decided the flag would make a perfect souvenir. He watched as two guards marched in perfect unity. First they marched away from the doorway in opposite directions and then turned and marched back together again. Louie counted the number of seconds the two guards had their backs to each other and the flag. He was sure it was enough time for him to run up, grab the flag, and make a quick escape.

Louie took a deep breath. As soon as the guards turned their backs to each other, he sprang into action. He jumped for the flag, but it was just out of reach. He tried again and again, totally forgetting that the guards were about to turn to face each other. When he finally caught the corner of the flag, he lost his balance and fell to the ground, pulling the flag down on top of him. With the flag in hand he jumped up and began to run.

Bang, the sound of a gun went off, and then the voice of one of the guards yelled, "*Halten sie! Halten sie!*"

By now Louie was thinking clearly enough to realize that even though he'd turned in the fastest 5,000-meter final lap ever recorded in Olympic history, he couldn't outrun a bullet. He stopped in his tracks.

A hand grabbed Louie's shoulder and swung him around. Louie came face-to-face with an angry Nazi guard. He was relieved to be wearing his Olympic uniform. He hoped the guard would think twice before roughing up an American athlete.

"Wait here," the second guard said, turning and marching inside.

As he waited with the first guard, Louie wondered what he had been thinking. How was he going to get himself out of this mess?

The second guard returned with another soldier, obviously an officer.

"Why did you want to steal that flag?" the officer demanded.

Louie smiled and spoke with an exaggerated American drawl. "I wanted somethin' to take home to always remind me I've had such a great time here. The German people have been so good to us, the ceremonies are amazing, everything's perfect. I just wanted a souvenir so I would never forget you all."

The officer grunted. "That is all?"

"Yes," Louie said. "Just a souvenir. I wasn't thinking. I'm sorry for the trouble I've caused."

"Ah, well," the officer said. "I can understand a young man wanting to remember the wonderful Berlin games." He waved at Louie. "Go and take the flag. But don't try this again. Most people trying to steal a flag from the Reich Chancellery are shot."

Louie grinned. "No, sir. Thank you, sir," he said, tucking the flag under his arm and walking away quickly. *This will make a great story when I get home,* he thought.

Chapter 8

SHATTERED DREAM

When the SS *Roosevelt* with the Olympic team aboard docked in New York, Louie learned that newspaper reporters had beaten him to telling his Nazi flag story.

"Boy, did they do a great job of making me look good!" he joked as he read several accounts in the newspapers.

One account had him fleeing in a hail of gunfire. In another he'd fallen eighteen feet after climbing for the flag. The best account of all said two columns of Nazi guards pursued Louie, caught him, confiscated the flag, and brought him to Hitler, who interrogated him and then handed the flag back to Louie.

So many people asked to see the flag that Louie began feeling a little edgy. Everyone seemed to know all about him. Now that he was an Olympic hero and with all these crazy stories swirling around him, he wondered how he was going to fit into regular life attending classes at USC.

Louie wanted a quiet homecoming and did not wire his parents that he was coming until the train reached Chicago. But the town of Torrance was determined to welcome home their "Tornado" in style. At Union Station in Los Angeles, Louie found Torrance's new police chief, John Strohe, waiting for him. Louie was bundled into the chief's cruiser, which took off, sirens blaring and lights flashing the entire thirty-mile trip home.

Entering the Torrance city limits, the cruiser stopped near a crowd. Louie thought there'd been an accident. He soon learned that the crowd was there for him. Louie was ordered out of the cruiser and onto a white throne on the back of a flatbed truck for a parade. Behind a fire truck a banner flew, declaring, "Zamperini Coming Home Tonight." Cars honked and the crowd chanted Louie's name.

At the town square a number of speeches were given. Chief Strohe got the biggest laugh when he patted Louie on the back and recounted how as a regular Torrance police officer he had often pursued Louie. "After I chased Louie up and down every back alley in Torrance, he had to be in shape for *something*," he said.

Weeks passed before Louie could make his way around Torrance without being stopped for a handshake or asked to tell a story about the Olympics.

When Louie started classes at USC, he was glad to be away from all the attention. Louie had decided to study physical education so he could become a high school PE teacher or work as a college coach. Things started well. He trained hard and made good enough grades.

While at USC Louie set his sights on breaking the world record for the National Collegiate Mile. Glenn Cunningham once held the record but was beaten by Bill Bonthron from Princeton University. Louie wanted to do better than Bill Bonthron, and his opportunity to do so came two years after returning from Berlin.

The USC track team traveled to Minneapolis, Minnesota, in June 1938 for the National Collegiate Athletic Association (NCAA) meet. Louie was in top physical shape, but competition in the mile race was going to be tough. He soon learned that some of the other runners would stop at nothing to see him lose.

Lying on the bed in his hotel room the night before the race, Louie was surprised by a knock at the door. "Come in," Louie called out. Coach John Nicholson from Notre Dame entered. Louie frowned. The coach was the last person he expected to see.

Shutting the door, Coach Nicholson said, "Louie, I'm sorry to have to say this, but I just came from the eastern coaches' meeting and your name came up. They're determined you're not going to win tomorrow. They're telling their boys to do whatever they have to do to take you out of the race. It's not about you. It's about your coach. They don't like him. Please be careful and protect yourself."

"I can take care of myself, sir," Louie said.

After Coach Nicholson left, Louie wondered if the coach had misunderstood the conversation among the eastern coaches. Louie had never seen a college runner do something to hurt another runner on the track. It just wasn't done.

The following day, during the mile race, Louie realized that Coach Nicholson hadn't misunderstood the conversation. Halfway through the race, a group of runners surrounded Louie and ran shoulder to shoulder with him, forcing him to run bunched up with no space to make a break for the lead. As they ran, one of the runners stomped on Louie's foot, spearing one of his toes with his running-shoe spikes. Louie winced in pain. Moments later the runner in front of him began kicking his feet back, his spikes slashing Louie's shins. Then the runner next to him elbowed him hard in the chest. Louie was shocked. He had no way to break free of the group, and he had to keep running with them. After a lap and a half, a small opening appeared in front of him. Louie bolted through it at full sprint, leaving the other runners behind and crossing the finish line in first place, his toe throbbing, shins bleeding, chest throbbing.

Louie was disappointed. It wasn't the race he had expected. He had wanted to set a new collegiate record for the distance, but given the interference on the track, he knew he must have posted a slow time. When he turned to see his official time on the scoreboard, Louie was dumbfounded. Despite the best efforts of other runners to thwart him, Louie had finished the mile in 4:08.3, the fastest mile in the history of the NCAA and the fifth fastest outdoor mile ever run. He was the fastest college miler in the United States, and he had missed the world record for the distance by 1.9 seconds. Louie learned after the race that the elbow to his chest had cracked one of his ribs.

Louie returned to USC a hero. His dream of becoming a gold medalist at the Tokyo Olympics was one step closer—or so he thought. Even though Louie was not particularly interested in world politics, he started paying attention to events in Japan. The year before, Japan had begun a massive and brutal invasion of China. This surprised Louie. The Japanese athletes he'd met in Berlin were warm and friendly.

Louie discussed the situation with one of his friends, Kunichi James Sasaki, whom everyone called Jimmie. Jimmie was one of Louie's fans, showing up at every track meet Louie competed in. He and Louie had something else in common. Although Jimmie had been born and raised in Japan, he loved Torrance, so much so that he apparently drove there almost every day to meet with people of Japanese descent, urging them to live good lives and to send relief money to their poor relatives in Japan. Louie found this a little confusing. He wondered why Jimmy picked Torrance to canvas. Not many people of Japanese descent lived there. But Jimmie wasn't one to answer questions about himself, though he certainly asked a lot of his own. And Jimmie wasn't much help to Louie in trying to understand why Japan had invaded China.

As the time for the next Olympic Games approached, Japan announced that it would not host them. The strain of Japan's invasion of China was apparently too much for the country to hold the Olympic Games. Fortunately, the Finnish government agreed to take on hosting the 1940 Olympic Games. But the clouds of war were gathering in Europe too. Germany had annexed Austria, invaded Czechoslovakia, and on September 1, 1939, invaded Poland. Two days later Britain, France, Australia, and New Zealand declared war on Germany.

Despite the change of venue for the Olympics and the troubling events going on around the world, Louie focused on his training and preparation. His times were getting faster. He won every race he entered, even beating his hero Glenn Cunningham twice and equaling the indoor mile record with a time of 4:07.9. Louie dreamed of beating the four-minute mile mark in Helsinki, Finland. His coach agreed he had a good chance of doing it.

It came as a shock in early 1940 when Louie learned that the Olympic Games in Helsinki were canceled. The Soviet Union, Germany's ally, had attacked Finland. In the process, the Olympic stadium had been bombed and partially collapsed. Louie was devastated, even more so when he learned that Gunnar Höckert, who had won the 5,000-meter gold medal in Berlin, had been killed defending his homeland. Louie could scarcely get his mind around the news. The world seemed to be descending into chaos.

For several days Louie walked around in a daze. Never in his wildest dreams could he have imagined the 1940 Olympic Games being canceled. Competing in those games was everything he'd worked for, everything he'd dreamed of. Who knew when the next games might be held—in four years, eight years? Louie would be too old to compete then. His chance at winning an Olympic gold medal was now, and that chance had evaporated before his eyes.

Following the cancellation of the Olympics, Louie's will to train lagged. He got food poisoning, and then pleurisy, and instead of winning races, he began to lose—all the time. He couldn't wait for the school year to end so he could leave.

In summer 1940, Louie landed a job as a welder at Lockheed Air Corporation in Burbank, California. The job wasn't much fun, but it put money in his pocket, and he had the satisfaction of helping the war effort. Even though the United States was officially neutral in the conflicts raging around the world, President Franklin Roosevelt was selling the P-38 fighter planes Louie was helping to build to the British Royal Air Force. The plane was also being used by the US Army Air Corps.

In September the Selective Training and Service Act was signed into law. This act required all American men between the ages of twenty-one and thirty-five to register with local draft boards. Men would be selected by a lottery system to train in the military for twelve months. Although not at war, the United States was gearing up for that possibility.

Twenty-three-year-old Louie didn't like the idea of leaving his fate to a lottery. He decided to select his own branch of the military to join before he could be drafted. Having watched countless P-38 fighters being test-flown at the adjacent airport, Louie decided to sign up for the Army Air Corps. He was assigned to Hancock College of Aeronautics in Santa Maria, California, for training.

Louie soon realized he'd made a big mistake. Flying airplanes made him queasy, and the spins made him throw up. Actually being in an airplane was not as much fun as Louie had thought when he watched the planes from the ground. Instead he found his fun elsewhere. Every weekend Louie and his new air corps buddies went into nearby San Luis Obispo, where they drank themselves into a stupor. Louie would straggle back to base and fall into his bunk, ready to do it all over again the next night.

With all the carousing, Louie had little time for study. Before long Louie was flunking his classes. Finally the Army Air Corps captain in charge of his training told Louie to either pull himself together or leave. Louie left, signing a discharge document he didn't even bother to read. He was a civilian again, but his fate still lay in the hands of the lottery draft system.

Louie returned home to live with his parents in Torrance. Because he couldn't even get his old job back as a welder at Lockheed, Louie earned a little money working as an extra in a Hollywood movie. The movie, titled *They Died with Their Boots On*, about the life of General Custer, was a big-budget movie starring Errol Flynn and Olivia de Havilland. Louie was paid seven dollars a day for his effort, with an additional twenty-five-dollar bonus if he stayed until the end of filming.

Staying to the end proved a problem. Before the movie finished filming, Louie was drafted. Not wanting to miss out on his bonus, he ran through various schemes in his mind to delay his military acceptance. He came up with a simple plan. On the day of his physical exam, Louie stuffed himself with as much candy as he could eat. When his urine was tested, the medical officer frowned. "Has anyone ever suggested you could have diabetes?" he asked.

"No, but I suppose it's possible," Louie replied with mock surprise. He knew the candy had raised his blood sugar level.

"We'll have to do the test again next week," the doctor said. "That way we'll know for sure. This result could be an aberration."

Louie nodded. "I'll come back," he said, knowing that the filming of the movie would be finished by then and he would get the extra twenty-five dollars.

Sure enough, when Louie's urine was tested a second time, his blood sugar level was normal, and on September 29, 1941, he reported for basic training at Camp Roberts, California. As he rode the train north from Torrance, Louie knew this time there was no way to flunk out of training.

While Louie was busy completing basic training, his brother Pete joined the US Navy.

At the end of basic training in November, Louie learned he should have read the paperwork he signed when he washed out of the Army Air Corps. Among the conditions he'd signed was one in which he agreed to rejoin the air corps should he be drafted. As much as he hated flying, Louie was assigned to Ellington Field in Houston, Texas. Like it or not, the Army Air Corps was going to make a bombardier out of him.

During bombardier training, Louie had a weekend pass for the sixth and seventh of December 1941. In the early morning hours of December 7, he was still in a movie theater watching a double feature when the movie suddenly stopped. Louie looked around to see what was going on as the lights came up and the theater manager walked out in front of the screen.

"The Japanese have bombed Pearl Harbor in Hawaii," the manager announced. "All military personnel are to return to their bases immediately."

Louie joined the stunned and silent stream of men and women leaving the theater. The United States had finally been drawn into the war raging on both sides of the globe. Louie wondered what this would mean for him and the country as he headed back to Ellington Field.

Chapter 9

COMBAT

Following the bombing of Pearl Harbor, Louie continued his bombardier training in Houston and then at the Army Flying School in Midland, Texas. He did well, learning to use the Norden bombsight, a secret, expensive, and sophisticated analog computer device. From his position in the greenhouse, the large Plexiglas window area at the front of a bomber, Louie learned how to locate the target with the bombsight, enter its position, and feed in other information using an array of knobs. The Norden bombsight, attached to the plane's autopilot, used the information to take over flying the bomber to the target. It also calculated the best angle and time to drop the bombs for maximum impact.

When the bombs were dropped, it was Louie's job to call "bombs away" so that the pilot could take over the controls again. Louie gained a reputation as an accurate bombardier using the bombsight. The Norden was designed for use when the bomber was flying level. Louie also learned to use a more primitive device consisting of an aluminum dial with pegs and a dangling weight to sight the target and manually release the bombs when the plane made a dive-bombing run.

In August 1942, his bombardier training over, Louie was commissioned a second lieutenant, assigned to the 372nd Bomb Squadron of the 307th Bomb Group, Seventh Air Force. He was ordered to report to the airbase at Ephrata in central Washington

State. He stopped in Torrance to visit his parents on the way. Pete was there too, and he and Louie swapped military stories. Pete was a chief petty officer in the navy, stationed at San Diego.

At his new posting in Ephrata, Louie was assigned to bomber crew number eight. The crew consisted of pilot Allen Phillips, copilot George Moznette Jr., engineer and top turret gunner Stanley Pillsbury, engineer and gunner at one of the two side-directed waist guns Clarence Douglas, navigator and nose gunner Robert Mitchell, tail gunner Ray Lambert, radio operator Frank Glassman, radio operator and other waist gunner Harry Brooks, and Louie as bombardier.

Louie hoped his crew would be assigned to a B-17 Flying Fortress bomber, but they got a B-24 Liberator. Louie's heart dropped as he stared at the new airplane, which looked ungainly. Some dubbed it a Flying Boxcar because of the squarish shape of its aluminum fuselage. The four-engine B-24 had a double tail, and while it was shorter than the B-17, its wingspan was wider. It was also lighter and faster and could fly farther than a B-17 and carry more bombs.

"They call these planes Flying Coffins," a ground crewman standing nearby said.

Allen Phillips, their pilot, a short man who didn't say much, spoke up. "Not for us, boys," he said to the crew. "It's a challenge, but one we can meet together."

The crew named their bomber *Super Man*, and within days they were making practice bombing runs. As they practiced together, Louie and the pilot struck up a warm friendship. It seemed like every crew member had his nickname, and Louie soon became Zamp while Allen Phillips answered to Phil.

After two months at Ephrata, the crew moved on to Sioux City, Iowa, for more training and more practice bombing runs. When their training was over, the men waited to see where they would be deployed. Would they be stationed in England, where the Allies were battling the Germans, or sent to the Pacific to do battle with the Japanese? By now the Japanese controlled large swaths of the Pacific and Asia. On November 2, 1942, Louie and the crew of *Super Man* found themselves flying west over the Pacific Ocean, headed for Hickam Field on the outskirts of Honolulu on the Hawaiian island of Oahu.

Louie was surprised when he arrived. Oahu was more like a fortress than a tropical paradise. Almost every building on the island seemed to be camouflaged, and the island was under a complete blackout. No light was permitted to be seen at night, not even a lit match. Barbed wire was strung along Waikiki Beach to keep any invading Japanese at bay. Louie had entered the war zone.

The 372nd Bomb Squadron was stationed at Kahuku Army Air Base, nestled beside the sea on the far northern tip of Oahu. It was a beautiful spot, and Louie liked to run around the runways to keep fit. At Kahuku the crew underwent more training, especially when George Moznette Jr. was transferred to another crew and Charleton Cuppernell took his place as copilot of *Super Man*. The crew also flew patterns back and forth across sectors of the Pacific Ocean off Hawaii searching for signs of Japanese ships or submarines. Flying search patterns up to ten hours at a time was tedious. Sometimes during these flights Phil let Louie take the plane's controls and gave him flying lessons. Surprisingly, given his first experience with the Army Air Corps, Louie grew to enjoy flying.

Like the rest of the crew, Louie longed for the combat action he'd been trained to carry out. The opportunity came on Christmas Eve 1942. The crews of twenty-five B-24 bombers were ordered to pack clothes for three days and report to their aircraft. *Super Man*'s crew gathered beside their plane and climbed aboard. Immediately Louie noticed that besides boarding six five-hundred-pound bombs in the bomb bay, the ground crew had installed two auxiliary fuel tanks. And to his surprise, the Norden bombsight wasn't in position for this mission. Louie would be relying on his handheld dive-bombing sight. Phil had been given a packet of orders but was forbidden to open it until after the plane had taken off. He was as clueless about the mission as Louie and the rest of the crew.

One after the other the bombers took off from Kahuku. As soon as *Super Man* reached a safe altitude, Phil opened the orders. The crew was to head to Midway Island, eight hours away. *Surely there must be more to it than just flying to Midway,* Louie thought as he settled in for the flight. And there was. After landing at Midway, the crews were informed that they were on their way to bomb Wake Atoll.

In December 1941 as they attacked Pearl Harbor, the Japanese had also attacked the US navy airbase on Wake Atoll, capturing it on December 23. In the year since, the Japanese had built a strategic airbase on Wake, and now twenty-five B-24 bombers were on their way to destroy what the Japanese had built.

The mission would push the B-24s to their limits. They would be in the air sixteen hours and have barely enough fuel to make it back to Midway. Now Louie knew why they needed auxiliary fuel tanks.

At four o'clock the following afternoon, *Super Man* and the other bombers took to the sky. One hundred fifty miles from Wake, under radio silence, the bombers switched off their outside lights. They were flying in clouds, and with no outside lights it was difficult to see the other bombers. Everyone on board knew there was a chance the planes would collide with each other before reaching the target.

The attack on Wake began at midnight. The planes lined up, and one after the other swooped in to drop their bombs. Louie opened the bomb bay doors and set his switches in preparation for their turn to dive in. The planes were supposed to drop the bombs from four thousand feet, but since they were still in clouds at that altitude, Phil kept heading down. At twenty-five hundred feet, Wake Atoll finally came into view. In the greenhouse at the front of the plane, Louie could see it all. Bombs from the previous planes had found their marks. Louie could see fires everywhere. He knew they'd caught the Japanese by surprise with their attack. He could make out Japanese soldiers running helter-skelter among the burning buildings and airplanes. He was close enough to see that most of them were in their underwear. *Super Man*'s gunners opened fire on the ground as Louie sighted his bombing targets and then sent the six bombs raining down. The bombs exploded on the runway and among parked Japanese aircraft, instantly setting them ablaze.

With their bombs dropped, Phil pulled the plane out of its dive, leveled off, and banked left, away from the burning atoll. With three thousand pounds of bombs gone from the bomb bay, *Super Man* was lighter and would be more fuel efficient for the return journey to Midway. Then Louie discovered that the bomb bay doors wouldn't close. One of the auxiliary fuel tanks had moved during the bombing run, jamming the doors. They would have to fly back to Midway with the doors open. The problem was, the open bomb bay doors created drag, causing *Super Man* to use more fuel than planned. They might not have enough fuel to make it back.

The return trip was nerve-wracking. Louie was glad for the fleece-lined jackets and boots the army issued the crew. Even though they were flying in the tropics, the altitude made them feel like they were riding in a refrigerator, and more so with the bomb bay doors wide open. Louie sat nervously watching the auxiliary fuel tank levels as the plane flew east.

Just after eight in the morning, Phil yelled to the crew that he could see Midway in the distance. At the same time, Louie heard one of the engines sputter and then die—it was out of fuel. Somehow the other three engines kept running. Louie was amazed. He could see there was no more fuel in the auxiliary tanks. He could feel when Phil dropped the bomber's nose and aimed at Midway's runway. Moments later the wheels thumped on the ground, just as another engine cut out. They had made it—barely. Louie knew that if the runway had been a half mile farther away, they would have crashed into the sea. He breathed a sigh of relief as the bomber taxied to a halt, just as its last two engines cut out.

When the mission was over, *Super Man* and all the other bombers participating in the raid on Wake Atoll returned safely.

Back on Oahu on New Year's Day 1943, Admiral Chester Nimitz presented Air Medals to the members of Louie's crew, along with the members of the other bomber crews involved in the raid. But Louie knew it was just as dangerous to participate in practice bombing runs as in actual combat. In his diary he kept a list of the airmen at Kahuku who'd been killed and how. It was sobering. By January 9, 1943, twenty-seven officers and twenty-six enlisted men had been lost. Some of them died when their planes smashed into the steep mountain ridges of Oahu or their planes blew up in midair from errant gas fumes. Some ran out of gas before reaching home and crashed, as *Super Man* nearly did returning to Midway. The gruesome story everyone talked about was an early-morning B-24 flight that crashed less than three hundred yards from shore. Several crew members survived and swam clear of the plane, only to be ripped apart by sharks before they reached the beach. Sharks were something Louie did not want to think about, but he knew they lurked in the endless blue seas they flew over.

Following that incident, Louie was sent to take a class from an old Hawaiian man on traditional ways to fend off shark attacks. In class they practiced opening their eyes wide and baring their teeth, as well as using the straight-arm technique, punching phantom sharks in the nose. Louie hoped he'd never have to find out whether or not the techniques worked.

With over a fourth of their barracks mates killed, Louie and the others developed a ritual to mark their passing. Since most of the time no body was found, the men opened the missing man's footlocker, found his alcohol supply, and drank a toast to his life. Then it was back to the business of staying alive themselves.

The next major battle *Super Man* was involved in came in mid-April 1943 with a bombing raid on the island of Nauru. In August 1942 the Japanese had occupied Nauru, a tiny island in the western Pacific just below the equator. Since the island was so remote and small, no one might have cared about the place, except for one thing—phosphate. Nauru had an abundant supply of top-grade phosphate that was used as an ingredient in the production of munitions, particularly incendiary bombs. The Japanese had established three phosphate-processing plants on the island, and the United States planned to destroy them.

The attack was carried out from the American airbase on Funafuti, a small atoll in the Ellice Islands about five hours' flying time southeast of Nauru. At five o'clock in the morning of April 20, 1943, twenty-two B-24 bombers, *Super Man* among them, took off from Funafuti. *Super Man* was to be the lead bomber on this raid. They took a longer, dogleg route to get to their target, hoping the Japanese could not track where they came from. At midday they were over Nauru, with *Super Man* the vanguard.

All seemed quiet three minutes before the bombing when Phil handed control of the plane to Louie, who set the coordinates for his targets into the Norden bombsight. Then a barrage of antiaircraft fire erupted from below. *Super Man* shuddered and rocked in the air from the percussion of the explosions around it but held its course, dropping its bombs on target. One of them hit a fuel dump, which exploded in a massive plume of red and orange. Following the bombing run, Phil took control of the plane, banked away from Nauru, and set course for Funafuti. But the Japanese weren't going to let them get away that easily. A dozen Japanese Zero fighters descended on the bombers, machine guns blazing.

Super Man was strafed with machine-gun fire from three Zeros. The bomber's guns opened fire on the Zeros. The noise was deafening. Louie watched as one Zero flew right at them. He heard a crack as a bullet from the fighter cut through the Plexiglas window right beside Louie's head and then exited and hit the left wing. Then through the shattered Plexiglas, Louie watched the Zero take a direct hit from nose gunner Robert Mitchell. He saw the pilot slump over and the plane fall away, spiraling down toward the ocean.

"Help!" a voice called over the intercom. A second volley of shells rocked *Super Man* as Louie rushed back to see what had happened. It was the stuff of nightmares. Harry Brooks, the radio operator, was dangling over the open bomb bay, clinging to the catwalk. His eyes were wild. Below him was a straight drop of eight thousand feet. Louie worked his way along the eleven-inch-wide catwalk until he was directly over the radio operator. He planted his feet firmly, reached down, grabbed Harry's wrists, and pulled him up onto the catwalk. Brooks was safe for the moment, but Louie realized they faced a new danger. A machine-gun bullet must have knocked out their hydraulic system, since Louie was sure he'd pushed the close button for the bomb doors after their run. This meant the flaps, landing gear, and brakes would all be out too.

Louie quickly hand cranked the doors shut and turned back to Harry, who was talking gibberish. Then Louie discovered why. Blood was pooling on the deck beside him. Harry had been hit in the stomach with shrapnel. Louie grabbed the first aid kit, gave Harry a shot of morphine, placed an oxygen mask over his face, and tried to stop the bleeding.

Boom! Louie heard a crack right above him, followed by a gooey, wet sensation on his neck. Was he bleeding? Louie looked up. Part of Stanley Pillsbury's boot had been torn apart by shrapnel, and blood flowed from Stanley's foot. But Stanley stayed at his post in the top gun turret.

The Zeros kept coming, and somehow *Super Man* kept flying through the hail of machine-gun fire.

Hearing more cries for help, Louie rushed to the back of the bomber. The sight that greeted him was unimaginable. Four crew members writhed in the waist gun section of the plane, bloody and wounded. Despite their injuries, Clarence Douglas and Frank Glassman were still at their waist gun positions.

Louie watched another Zero careen toward them. He wasn't sure *Super Man* could stand another attack. But Stanley was ready for it. Despite his shrapnel-mangled foot, he waited for his moment and then let out a yell of anger and opened fire. Louie could see the Japanese pilot dead in his cockpit as the Zero suddenly dropped below them out of control.

The fight for them was over, but six crewmen were badly injured, and the plane was hardly fit to fly. Louie didn't have time to think about how they would land safely, even if they were able to reach land. He had to work on his crewmates. He reached up and gave Stanley a shot of morphine in the leg, then sprinkled sulfur powder on his foot and bandaged it.

Copilot Charleton Cuppernell made his way back to Louie, and the two of them tended to the injured while Phil struggled to keep the mangled plane in the air. Besides the hydraulic system being ruptured, one of the tail rudders had been shot off. Somehow *Super Man* kept flying. It was the longest five hours of Louie's life as he waited for Funafuti to come into view. But a crash landing seemed inevitable. Without hydraulics, they had to hand crank the flaps and landing gear into position. Next Louie opened the bomb bay doors to create drag, hoping it would help slow the plane. With that accomplished, all Louie could do was wonder how, with no brakes, Phil would stop *Super Man* after they touched down.

A bullet had punctured the tire on the left wheel, and the plane veered dangerously left after touchdown. Louie was certain they were done, that they would be torn apart by the fast-approaching coconut trees. He watched Charleton stomp on the right brake. To Louie's amazement there was just enough hydraulic pressure left for the right brake to lock and spin *Super Man* in the opposite direction before it came to an abrupt halt next to the runway.

Louie leapt to the ground through the bomb bay doors and raised his arms to make a cross, the sign they had wounded aboard. Marines with stretchers came running, and the injured crewmen were handed off to them.

As he walked around *Super Man*, Louie marveled that he was still alive. The bomber's fuselage and wings had 594 bullet holes in them. Every B-24 that took part in the Nauru raid made it back to Funafuti. Each bomber was damaged from bullets and shrapnel, but none as badly as *Super Man*.

Before nightfall, Harry Brooks died of his injuries. Louie would never forget the pleading look in Harry's eyes as he pulled him away from the open bomb bay. Wanting to be alone, Louie walked over to a grove of coconut trees. He watched numbly as ground crewmen busily repaired the damaged bombers, refueling them and loading them with more bombs. In the morning the planes would take off on another mission, this time over Tarawa in the Gilbert Islands, where the Japanese were entrenched. But *Super Man* wouldn't be joining them. The plane was too badly damaged to repair. It would never fly again.

Exhausted, Louie headed to a barracks tent and lay on a cot. He drifted into a restless sleep, the events of the day still playing in his mind. Around four o'clock in the morning he awoke to the sound of aircraft overhead. Louie assumed they were American planes bringing in reinforcements, but he soon realized he was wrong. He heard one explosion, and then another.

"Air raid!" someone yelled.

Louie leapt from his cot, pulled on his boots, and ran outside. Explosions were lighting the sky on the other end of the atoll.

"Where are the bomb shelters?" Louie yelled.

"There aren't any. Just do your best," someone yelled back.

Louie thought quickly. He knew that he and the other men on the atoll were sitting ducks. He had to get as low to the ground as possible. He spotted a native hut on stilts a short distance away. He ran for it and dived under the structure. Phil was right behind him. A dozen other men were already in there, and Louie piled on top of them. More airmen tumbled in. Louie covered his ears with his hands, curled up, and braced for impact. The ground quaked beneath them with each exploding bomb.

The Japanese made four bombing runs over Funafuti, and once more Louie lived up to his nickname, Lucky Louie. The hut he'd taken shelter under was not hit. All he suffered was a minor cut to his arm.

As daylight broke, Louie emerged. All around him acrid smoke swirled upward from burning B-24s and buildings. Men lay dead amid the chaos. Bits of clothing were mangled together with airplane pieces and truck parts. Palm trees were shredded. Men screamed in pain. Louie shook as he took in the scene. To the left he spotted *Super Man*, the only bomber that hadn't been hit in the air raid. The plane still sat beside the runway where it had spun to a stop.

Later in the morning Louie went to the infirmary to check on *Super Man*'s injured crewmen. They had all made it through the attack. When Louie checked in on Stanley Pillsbury, however, the doctor had bad news. There was no more anesthetic, but Stanley's foot needed immediate attention. Louie volunteered to help. While Stanley gripped the side of his cot, Louie lay across his legs to hold them still. The doctor went to work. Beneath him Louie could feel Stanley's body tense up with pain. After cleaning the wound, the doctor stitched Stanley's foot back together.

By the time Louie left the infirmary, he wondered how he would ever get the gruesome images of the past two days out of his head.

Chapter 10

THE *GREEN HORNET*

The crew of *Super Man* would never be a team again. Stanley Pillsbury, Ray Lambert, and Clarence Douglas were too injured to move. The others, including Louie, were flown from Funafuti back to Hawaii. Once back in Hawaii, Louie, Phil, and Charleton were transferred to the 42nd Squadron of the 11th Bombing Group, stationed at Kualoa Army Airfield, situated beside the ocean on the east coast of Oahu. There they met the six other men who would be their new crewmen. Louie was a little nervous. *Super Man*'s crew had been battle tested. Now they would have to build that trust again with a new group of men, some rookies, like their new engineer. To make matters worse, the reformulated crew had no aircraft to fly. The men waited for a new bomber from the mainland.

Meanwhile on Thursday morning, May 27, 1943, Louie, Phil, and Charleton headed to Honolulu to buy supplies. They were about to leave base when Lieutenant Lund, the operations officer, stopped them at the gate.

"I need some volunteers immediately," the lieutenant said, walking up to the driver's side window of the car. "You boys look like you don't have much to do."

"What's the problem?" Louie asked.

"A B-24 is missing. It took off yesterday afternoon for Australia via Palmyra and hasn't been heard of since. We need to put two planes in the air to search for it."

"No use talking to us, sir," Phil said. "We don't have a plane anymore."

"Take the *Green Hornet*," the lieutenant replied.

Louie shot Phil an alarmed look. The *Green Hornet*, a B-24 bomber, was the dud of the squadron. Pilots who flew the plane reported it was hard to control. It was a "musher," that is, its tail sagged lower than its nose during flight. Worse, the maintenance crew had been pulling parts from it to use on other planes. When the bomber was used, it was usually to fly to the big island of Hawaii to pick up cabbages and other produce to bring back to Oahu.

Phil spoke up. "I'll fly anything but that plane," he said.

"The *Green Hornet* is the only spare plane available. It's passed inspection. I need a volunteer crew now—are you going to do it or is there going to be trouble?" Lieutenant Lund demanded.

Louie sighed.

"Of course, we're going to do it," Phil said.

In the military the word *volunteer* had a different meaning. If the plane had passed inspection, they had no choice but to fly it. The three men turned the car around. Their day in Honolulu was canceled. It was time to take their chances with the *Green Hornet*.

Louie changed into his uniform and made a quick entry in his journal. "There was only one ship, the Green Hornet. . . . We were very reluctant, but Philips finally gave in for the rescue mission." He put the journal back in his footlocker, scribbled a note, and left it on top. "If we're not back in a week, help yourself to the booze."

Two hours later the *Green Hornet* was flying toward Palmyra Atoll, just above the equator, a thousand miles south of Hawaii. Louie felt uneasy. The plane had six new crew members aboard, as well as an officer hitching a ride to Palmyra. Louie wondered whether in an emergency the men would be able to function as a team. He took a deep breath and hoped they wouldn't have to find out.

Another B-24 bomber, the *Daisy Mae*, was also searching for the downed plane, and the two planes flew together for the first two hundred miles until the *Daisy Mae* went on ahead, since the *Green Hornet* lumbered along so slowly.

Louie surmised they'd reached the search area, about two hundred miles from Palmyra, when the *Green Hornet* ducked beneath a cloud layer. He guessed they were skimming over the ocean about eight hundred feet up. As Louie scanned the calm sea below with his binoculars, he felt sorry for the missing crew. He hoped they'd made it into life rafts.

"Take a look dead ahead, would you?" Phil said.

Louie stood at the back of the cockpit. As he scanned the sea, he felt a surge of relief that Phil was in charge. If anyone could fly this old bucket of bolts, Phil could. After all he'd managed to keep the badly damaged *Super Man* aloft for five hours on the way back to Funafuti.

"Can we switch seats?" Louie heard Charleton ask Phil.

Phil unbuckled his seatbelt. "Sure," he answered.

Louie stood behind the pilot and copilot as they changed places. It was a common occurrence since most copilots wanted as many hours as possible in the captain's chair to earn their own captain's qualifications.

Louie and Phil were chatting when, without warning, Louie felt a shudder. He looked to his left. Engine Number 1, on the far end of the wing, was sputtering and shaking. Then the engine conked out. Immediately the *Green Hornet* began to tip left and lose altitude. Louie stood back to let Phil and Charleton take charge. They had to reduce drag on the left side of the plane by feathering the propeller blades of the stalled engine. This meant turning the blade edge to the wind to stop the propeller's turning and allow the blades to cut through the air with as little resistance as possible. Feathering the propeller was normally the copilot's job, but since Phil and Charleton had switched seats, they seemed to Louie to be a little disoriented. Louie heard Phil yell for their engineer to come feather the blades on the disabled engine.

The rookie engineer raced to the cockpit, leaned across the instrument console, flipped open the plastic lid covering four buttons, and hit the button to feather the propeller blades on the stalled Number 1 engine. In a flash Louie realized that the engineer had hit the wrong button. The Number 2 engine of the left side had stopped dead. The *Green Hornet* now had both its left engines out. The plane could barely fly with four engines working, and Louie could see the shock on Phil's face. Phil increased power to the two right engines to compensate while Charleton tried to restart the Number 2 engine. With no running engines on the left side, the *Green Hornet* began to spin in that direction. The plane was quickly running out of altitude as it plummeted.

"Prepare to crash," Louie heard Phil yell into the intercom.

Louie leapt into action. He'd gone over this moment a hundred times in survival class, and thousands more in his head. Each crew member had a specific job to do at that moment. The bomber was fitted with two life rafts that would launch and inflate automatically after a crash. A third life raft was located in the bomb bay, and it was Louie's job to retrieve it and then take his position by the right waist window beside the machine-gun tripod mount. Louie dashed to the bomb bay and grabbed the life raft. The *Green Hornet* was now spiraling out of control.

Louie saw their new tail gunner, Sergeant Francis McNamara, whom everyone called Mac, holding the survival provisions box, as was his role. He heard someone behind him struggling with his life vest. Louie was glad he'd strapped his on before the plane took off. He was vaguely aware that he hadn't seen the radio operator running to his position. He hoped he was running through his emergency sequence, sending out a distress signal and strapping a sextant and celestial navigation kit to his body.

There's nothing more I can do, Louie thought as he dropped to the floor. He took one last look at the sky out the waist window, tucked his head into his chest, and pulled the uninflated life raft over his head. As the *Green Hornet* screamed toward the water, Louie thought, *So this is how it ends? Nobody's going to live through this.*

Bang! Louie's world exploded. He saw daylight overhead as he was flung forward. Water engulfed him as cords wrapped around his torso. In an instant Louie was facedown, wedged beneath the machine-gun mount. Louie clawed at the tangle of cords, but he had no way to free himself. The fuselage began to sink toward the seafloor seventeen hundred feet below. Louie gulped in salt water and gagged. He needed air, but there was none. His lungs were beginning to fill with water, and then everything went dark as he blacked out.

Seconds later Louie came to. His world was dim, cold, and silent. He was floating. Was this death? As the thought flashed through Louie's mind, the throb from his ears overtook it. A thumping pressure in his eyes felt like a hammer hitting an anvil. Louie realized that he was alive and floating free inside the fuselage. He had no idea how he got free, but the wires no longer entangled him, and he wasn't wedged under the gun mount.

Louie ran his hands along the fuselage looking for a way out. He found the opening of the waist window and ran his right hand along the edge of it. His USC ring caught fast on some twisted metal. Louie used his left hand to pull himself to the window. He forced his body through the hole and yanked his right hand free, cutting his finger.

Placing both feet on the edge of the window, Louie launched himself toward the surface. He pulled the cord on his life vest to inflate it, its buoyancy pulling him up faster and faster. Louie broke the surface gasping for air. He took a gulp of air, then vomited up a mixture of sea water and aviation oil. He took another breath and looked around. The sea was a soup of plane parts and fiery debris.

"Help!" someone yelled. Louie turned and saw Phil and Mac clinging to a twisted, buoyant chunk of metal. Even at twenty yards Louie could see that Phil had a gash over his eye. Mac was staring vacantly into the ocean. Louie knew someone needed to stop Phil's bleeding, but as he looked around, he saw two yellow inflated life rafts quickly floating away in the current. With no life rafts they were doomed. The metal the other two clung to would soon sink, and they would be treading water in the vast Pacific Ocean. And with Phil's bleeding wound, sharks would not take long to find them.

With a spurt of adrenalin, Louie swam for the first raft. But the current carried it along faster than he could swim. It was hopeless, or at least he thought it was until something wiggled in front of him. It was the nylon release cord trailing behind the raft. Louie grabbed the cord, wound the end around his hand, and began to pull the raft toward him.

Louie hoisted himself into the raft, glanced back at Phil and Mac, took the oars, and rowed as hard as he could after the other life raft. With two rafts they would have twice the provisions and twice as much room to move about in. When Louie reached the second raft, he lashed the two rafts together and headed back for the other men.

Mac was able to pull himself over the side of the raft, and Louie hauled Phil aboard. Amazingly Mac hadn't been hurt at all. Mac ripped off his shirt. Louie dipped it in sea water and held it tight against Phil's forehead with his right hand while using his left hand to press down hard on Phil's carotid artery. All he could do was hope it was enough to stop the bleeding.

Phil looked up at Louie through hazy eyes. "Zamp," he said. "Take over. You're the captain now."

"Sure," Louie replied. "Take it easy. Don't worry. We'll be picked up soon."

Louie wasn't lying. He believed his words. He knew that they had crashed on the well-flown route between Hawaii and Palmyra Atoll. When the *Daisy Mae* landed at Palmyra and the *Green Hornet* didn't, it wouldn't take long for people to realize that the plane was missing. All Louie had to do was keep Phil alive until they heard the buzz of a rescue aircraft.

It was several hours before the shirt wrapped around Phil's head stopped seeping blood. Phil was resting in the second raft while Mac and Louie sat together in silence in the other one.

Suddenly Mac yelled, "We're going to die! We're all going to die!"

Louie was stunned. They were the lucky ones so far, and he chose to believe their luck would last.

"No we're not, Mac," Louie said soothingly. "We're all fine. We'll be picked up today or tomorrow at the latest. Hang in there, buddy."

"We're all going to die," Mac continued yelling again and again.

Louie tried to reason with Mac, but it was useless. Finally he reached over and slapped Mac across the face. Mac fell silent, and his eyes glazed over.

"Let's see what we have here," Louie said to change the subject.

He turned out his pockets. He had several quarters and pennies along with his wallet. He then untied the side pocket inside the life raft and pulled out the emergency pack. Inside he found four half-pint canteens of water, three large Hershey Ration D chocolate bars, two air pumps in canvas bags, a pair of pliers with one handle fashioned into a screwdriver, a brass mirror, flare guns, sea dye, a kit for patching leaks, and some fishhooks and line. The emergency pack in the second raft had the identical provisions.

Louie was stunned. Where was the knife? Where was the first aid kit? And how long would eight half-pints of water and six Hershey bars last them? He thought of all the things he could have shoved into his pockets before leaving that morning: the canteen silverware, a roll of bandages, a flashlight, some dried fruit, even a good book.

As he felt panic and fear begin to rise, Louie checked himself. *We won't be here long,* he told himself. He felt sorry for anyone who ended up on a B-24's life raft for more than forty-eight hours. It would be tough to survive on what they had to work with. Louie decided that after they were rescued and got back to base, he would write some recommendations for what else to include among the life raft's survival equipment.

Chapter 11

ADRIFT

Nineteen-ten," Louie told Mac as he watched a spectacular sunset. "The sun goes down at nineteen-ten." It was good to know the time. Louie's watch was still on his wrist, but it had stopped at the moment of the crash. "The alert will be out for us now. Planes will be looking when the sun comes up. That's only about ten hours away. We'll be rescued tomorrow."

Louie was watching the last rays of sun dance across the water when a triangular shape moved silently toward them. Then another came up beside it. Louie let out a long breath—sharks! *Stay calm,* he told himself. *You're in the raft, they're outside it.* But it was hard for Louie to keep his mind from running to the shark stories he'd heard back on Oahu, stories of the men ripped apart after their plane crashed just off the end of the runway, the airman whose leg was bitten off as he sacrificed himself to the sharks so his buddy could swim for shore.

The sharks, three of them, glided up to the raft, and then Louie's hair stood on end. They were swimming under it. Louie could feel their fins rubbing against the raft bottom. He remained still. Less than an eighth of an inch separated them—two layers of canvas coated in yellow rubber. The raft was sturdy, but Louie was sure that a shark could puncture it with one snap of its jaw. The sky grew black. It was a moonless night, but Louie could feel the sharks circling, dipping under the raft, and circling again.

As he sat nervously, Louie could hear Phil's teeth chattering. The night was cold, and the temperature was dropping by the minute. Remembering a tip from survival training, Louie used the sea anchor, a long rectangular canvas pouch, to scoop six inches of water into each raft. Their bodies would warm the water around them. Exhausted, Louie lay in the raft beside Mac as the slosh of waves lulled him to sleep. For the first time he was able to concentrate on his body. He had tried to ignore the jabbing pains in his chest, but now, as he felt around his rib cage, Louie was sure he'd broken several ribs. And his back stung in the salt water where the skin was scraped off.

Louie also had time to think about the crash. When the double tail ripped off on impact, the rubber control wires had snapped. The tension had recoiled them back down the fuselage, and the wires had wrapped hopelessly around him. Louie played the scene of his escape over and over in his head. He could think of no logical reason why he was untangled from the wire spaghetti wrapped around him, why he came to after blacking out, and why he was no longer pinned under the gun mount. There was no explanation. All Louie could come up with was that God was watching out for him. It was a conclusion he would have scoffed at two days ago. Now it seemed as good an explanation as any.

When the sun arose, Louie was grateful. It had been a cold night. He looked around at the endless ocean. The triangular fins swerving left and right around the raft told him the sharks were still trailing them.

"Friday, May 28th," Louie announced loudly. "Today's the day they find us." He then felt the urge to do something he hadn't done since he was a little boy attending Mass. "Let's pray, boys," he said.

The other two men nodded. Louie knew Phil's father was a

Methodist minister, but he and Phil had never talked about faith in God. Now Louie was ready to ask for any kind of help he could get.

"Our Father who art in heaven, hallowed be thy name," Louie began. Phil and Mac joined in.

When they finished reciting the Lord's Prayer, Louie announced it was time for breakfast. Untying the life raft pocket, he reached in to pull out the first bar of the Hershey chocolate. He salivated at the thought of food. His hand felt around. No bars. He tried the next compartment. Still none.

Louie frowned. He knew he'd put the bars back in the pocket last night. Where could they be? They couldn't have washed overboard. Louie looked at the other two men. Phil lay exactly where he'd been the night before, his head encased in a bloodied shirt. Louie looked at Mac, who stared expressionless. In a flash he knew that Mac had eaten all the chocolate bars in the night.

"What did you do?" Louie whispered to Mac so as not to upset Phil. "What did you do?"

Mac shrugged and stared out to sea.

Louie resisted the urge to punch Mac in the face, but what Mac had done was unthinkable. "Why?" he asked.

Mac didn't answer.

"I don't know anyone who'd do that. We're supposed to be a team. We're in this together," Louie hissed.

Mac continued staring into the water, and Louie stopped talking. He told himself it didn't matter much. They would be rescued today. By nightfall they'd all be dining in a mess hall.

As his anger subsided, Louie began to feel sorry for Mac. *It's all in your head. You win or lose the race in your head first.* Louie could almost hear Pete saying the words to him. As he reflected, he knew the words were as true in a raft as they were on the track. At twenty-three years of age, Mac was the youngest of the three men. He was the only one to come through the crash unscathed, yet Louie could see that if things went on much longer, Mac was the one who would crack up.

Slowly Louie realized he was hearing something over the slosh of the waves against the raft. Was it a droning sound? He sat up. The others had heard it too, and they began scanning the sky.

"One of our B-25s!" Louie exclaimed, looking east. "It's high. It can't be searching for us, but still . . ." He grabbed a flare gun from the raft pocket, loaded it, and shot off a flare. A red arch lit the sky. Louie pulled out a dye pack, ripped it open with his teeth and emptied it into the water. Immediately a large yellow circle of dye surrounded them. The men waved and yelled. The plane flew on.

"We're headed west," Phil croaked.

Louie nodded. "Looks like it," he said, realizing the plane was probably on a routine flight between Hawaii and Palmyra. It was well to the east, which meant they were drifting away from that well-flown corridor.

Louie imagined a map of the Pacific Ocean. Their situation wasn't good. The spot where they were floating was right in the middle of the widest span of the Pacific, over twelve thousand miles across. The next solid ground to the east was South America, and to the west the Philippines and Southeast Asia. They were sitting on two small rafts in the widest stretch of the largest ocean on earth. They were weeks, maybe months, away from land. But could they hold out that long? Louie didn't want to think about that.

"We're alive now," Louie mumbled quietly to himself. "That's what matters."

An hour later, with the sun beating down relentlessly, Louie told Phil about the fate of the chocolate ration bars. Phil didn't react, which was no surprise to Louie, who had never seen Phil angry. It was one of the things that made Phil such a good pilot.

"How about fishing?" Phil asked.

"No bait," Louie replied, feeling a bump on the bottom of the raft. The sharks were back. Louie leaned over the side and saw the tail of what he thought was a mako shark surrounded by small pilot fish.

There were no more airplane sightings that day, and the men retreated into their own worlds. Phil slipped in and out of sleep, Mac lay staring at the water, and Louie closed his eyes and thought of the endless buffet he had enjoyed aboard the SS *Manhattan* on his way to the Olympic Games in Berlin.

Another night descended, and Louie bailed more water into each raft to keep them warm. He was very hungry by now and struggling to forgive Mac for eating the chocolate bars. Louie was carefully meting out the drinking water, but even at a few sips a day, they would soon be out.

During the following day they sang a lot. Louie loved the latest Bing Crosby show tunes, while Phil taught them Methodist hymns. Louie sang, "Guide me, O Thou great Jehovah, pilgrim through this barren land," while sitting on a raft surrounded by sixty-four million square miles of water. Still, he did feel like a pilgrim in a strange and distant place and sang heartily the line "Feed me till I want no more" as a prayer. He tried to keep up hope that one day their stomachs would be full again.

Not long after they finished singing, Louie heard the sound of thundering engines above. He scanned the sky just as a B-24 bomber broke through the clouds. It was so close the men could see their squadron insignia on the tail. With a whoop of joy, Louie grabbed the flare gun and shot it off. All three men watched as the flare arched overhead and then exploded near the plane.

"They had to see that!" Phil said jubilantly.

Just to be sure, Louie fired three more flares. The plane banked right. It was turning around. Then having seen the plane complete the turn, the castaways watched as the bomber droned on, getting smaller and smaller in the sky.

"Why didn't they see us?" Louie fumed. "The lookouts weren't doing their job. It was impossible to miss us!"

The men had now used up four flares and still had not been spotted. Louie felt a flash of doubt. Perhaps they wouldn't be rescued after all. It was time to switch from thinking about rescue to concentrating on surviving—possibly for a long time.

That night, which Phil remembered was Memorial Day, the men drank the last drops of water. Louie knew how desperate the situation was. He imagined what was going on back on Oahu. The search for them had probably been called off by now, and his friends would have opened the footlocker, found his note, and drank a toast to him and Phil. The rest of his belongings, including his diary, would be shipped home to his parents. A "missing in action" telegram would also be delivered to the Zamperini home in Torrance. Louie could hardly imagine what the family would think when they got the telegram. His mother would be heartbroken.

"We're doomed!" Mac's voice broke the silence. "We are all going to die. We'll never see land again. It's impossible to survive."

"Quiet, Mac," Louie said. "That's no way to think. We won't make it unless we think we can. You've got to be hardy."

"We're going to die," Mac screamed. "Admit it, Zamperini. We're all going to die."

"Enough," Louie said, but Mac kept ranting. Once again Louie slapped him hard across the face. Mac fell back, cowering like a beaten dog.

Louie sat watching the whitecaps and thinking about being hardy. It was a quality that separated men from boys during war. Everyone got the same training and had the same equipment, but when push came to shove, some men could stuff their fears away and get on with the job of survival, while others, like Mac, couldn't. It all came down to how hardy you were. For once Louie was glad for his early years as a juvenile delinquent. They had made him scrappy, able to think quickly and logically without panicking. Now, he hoped, those same traits would not desert him. He had to find a way to get food and water—soon.

Another day followed, and then another. The sharks stayed with the rafts. Mac alternated between lying sullenly in the bottom of the raft and sitting up yelling about dying. Phil started to regain his strength, and he and Louie marked their time by the sun's position in the sky. They also watched constantly for any sign of rain-bearing clouds. There were none.

As Louie sat in the raft, his mind drifted back to Dr. Roberts, his physiology professor at USC. Dr. Roberts had often told the class, "Your mind is everything. It's like a muscle. You must use it, or it will waste away, just like a muscle." Louie was sure this was true, and he set about keeping their minds sharp and active.

He turned to Phil. "Hey, buddy, tell me about what it's like to grow up in Indiana. What did you do for fun when you were a kid?"

Phil smiled. "No place like it," he said. "The most fun we had was going to the Indianapolis 500. We'd take lunch and spend the whole day there. I'll never forget when Louis Meyer won for the third time . . ."

On and on the stories went. Louie retold every incident he could remember from his turbulent childhood. Phil countered with stories about being a preacher's son. They turned their attention to the future. Louie described his dream to turn the train depot in Torrance into a fancy restaurant, while Phil talked of marrying his sweetheart Cecile and becoming a science teacher.

Along with the reminiscing, Phil and Louie held countless quiz contests, with Mac occasionally joining in. No topic was too small to be explored in great detail. After all, they had nothing but time. The men relived their best dates, their funniest practical jokes, the books and magazines they'd read as children, the classes they'd taken at college. It didn't take Louie long to realize that Phil was much more of a scholar than he was. Phil had earned a degree in forestry and conservation at Purdue University, and Louie learned a lot from him about saplings, invasive species, and the role of fire in forests.

Through all the talk, though, the thought of food and drink was never far from Louie's mind. "You know, my mother was the best cook," he told the other men. "Boy, I can see her now in the kitchen, mixing up a batch of gnocchi."

"I haven't heard of that. How did she make it?" Phil asked.

"Well, boys," Louie said, "let's start at the beginning. First off you need a couple of pounds of old potatoes—not new ones, old ones with lots of starch in them."

"Okay," Phil said.

"Then you peel the potatoes and boil them."

"Do you add salt?" Phil inquired.

It took Louie ten minutes to explain the ins and outs of making gnocchi, and when he was finished, Phil wanted him to explain how to cook the blue cheese sauce his mother made to go with it.

That afternoon began a tradition. Three times a day, breakfast, lunch, and dinner, Louie would conjure up a meal, recounting exactly how it was made, while Phil and Mac listened intently. If he forgot to beat an egg before adding it to the carbonara or indent the gnocchi with the back of a fork before boiling it, Louie heard about it.

The men were desperately thirsty by now, and although they could distract themselves with imaginary meals, it wasn't hard to see that they were losing weight fast. Every other day Louie had to cinch up his belt a notch, and Phil's face looked long and gray. Phil's eyes were dull too, which bothered Louie.

On the morning of June 2, 1943, when the three men had been in the rafts for five days, Louie spotted a tiny cloud forming on the horizon. It grew bigger and floated toward them. They stopped talking as it came overhead, blotting out the sun for one glorious minute. Then a drop fell, and another. It was raining! Louie threw his head back, laughing and opening his mouth to catch the fresh, cool water. He pulled off his shirt, allowing the water to wash his sticky, salty skin.

As the rain fell, Louie knew he had to find a way to collect it. The half-pint water canteens were useless. Their tops were hardly larger than a quarter. He felt around in the pocket for something else to use. He pulled out the air pumps. Each one was in a canvas pouch. Louie quickly ripped the seam along the side of each pouch to make a canvas bowl. He gave one bowl to Mac and held the other one up to the rain.

It felt too good to be true—and it was. A large wave crashed over the raft, mixing sea water with the rainwater in the canvas pouch. Louie threw the water overboard and started again. This time, he'd have to think of some way to protect the fresh water. He waited until an inch had gathered in the bottom of the pouch, then he sucked his cheeks full of rainwater, took the lid off the water canteen, and spat it into the canteen. It wasn't the most hygienic thing to do, but it worked. Before the cloud had rained itself out, all eight half-pint canteens were full.

The men also took turns using the two canvas pouches as hats. The hats helped a little to keep the searing sun off their blistered and swollen lips.

On their ninth day in the rafts, Louie was sitting with one of the canvas pouches on his head when an albatross landed on it. The bird, not realizing it was sitting on a man, perched contentedly as Louie slowly raised his hand until it was beside the creature. In a flash Louie closed his hand around the albatross's legs. The bird put up a fight, but Louie wrestled it, eventually snapping its neck.

Louie used the pliers to tear the albatross apart. The bird stank as Louie pulled off chunks of raw meat and handed them to Phil and Mac to eat. The truth was, the albatross smelled so bad that none of them—not even Louie—could eat the meat. Instead Louie decided to use the raw meat as bait. He took out the hooks, tied one to the line, baited it, and lowered it over the side. Almost immediately a shark swam by, swallowing the bait and hook. Louie attached another hook with bait and lowered it over the side. Another shark gobbled the hook and bait. Louie tried again, and again another shark swam in and snatched the bait. On the fourth try, the sharks left the bait and hook alone, and moments later Louie pulled in a pilot fish. Even Louie had to admit it wasn't much of a fish. Once again he used the pliers to tear the creature apart. Although the raw fish tasted bland, it didn't stink like the albatross and was soon reduced to a pile of bones.

Life on the rafts was monotonous. The only difference between days was the ocean itself. Sometimes the swell was so high the rafts felt like a roller coaster, riding up a swell, then plummeting down the other side. Other times the ocean was as calm as a pond, and Louie could hear a fish jump out of the water 150 feet away.

As each day passed, the men wasted away. Huge boils and salt blisters covered Louie's body, his teeth ached, and the lining of his mouth became so swollen he could barely swallow. Sleep was also hard to come by. It was too hot during the day and too cold at night. When Louie did manage to sleep, he dreamed of lying on hard surfaces—a woodpile, a roof, it didn't seem to matter as long as the surface was solid. Louie also dreamed of food, not the banquets and buffets he'd attended, but the food he used to throw onto the compost heap when he was a boy—apple cores, banana peels, pea shells. What he wouldn't give to have those scraps now!

The thirteenth day after the crash, Wednesday, June 9, Louie remembered it was his father's fifty-fourth birthday. He wondered what his parents were doing. He wondered about his sisters. Most of all Louie wondered about his brother Pete. What was he up to? Was he in Europe or the Pacific? And then there was the question Louie tried not to dwell on: Was Pete alive or dead?

The next day a second albatross landed on the raft. Once again Louie managed to catch the unsuspecting bird. This albatross didn't smell as bad as the first one, and they all ate its flesh. Louie and Phil poured the bird's blood into Mac's mouth, since Mac was the weakest. Louie was grateful that the albatross had small fish in its stomach. He used the fish as bait. Louie was able to catch one larger fish, which the men also ate.

When the canteen water supply ran dry again, Louie began to doubt they'd survive. He thought back to when he first arrived in Hawaii and Eddie Rickenbacker, the World War I ace pilot, and his crew had just been rescued. Their B-17D Flying Fortress had run out of gas and gone down in the Central Pacific during a tour of the

Pacific air bases. Rickenbacker and his crew had set a record of twenty-one days drifting on rafts much like the one Louie was in. When the men were picked up, they were dehydrated, hallucinating, and near death. Louie was sure that twenty-one days on a life raft represented the outer limits of human survival.

Chapter 12

LAND AT LAST!

B y the fifteenth day in the raft, Louie's body cried for water. His lips were so swollen that his top lip touched his nose, his feet were swollen, and his throat was so raspy that he could barely talk. There was nothing he could do except pray.

"Hey, fellows," he rasped to the others. "How about we pray for water?"

"Okay," croaked Phil.

Mac nodded.

Louie prayed. "God, we need water soon. Please send us water. If You answer my prayers now and save us, I'll seek You and serve You the rest of my life." Louie knew it sounded like he was bargaining with God, and he hoped that God would understand.

An hour later a tiny cloud appeared on the horizon. It rapidly blew across the sky until it was over the rafts. Then rain began to fall—lots of it. Louie let out a whoop of delight and held his mouth up to the drops falling from the sky. Then he reached up with the canvas pump bag to catch the precious liquid.

Several days later, when their fresh water was again running out, Louie prayed once more, and the same thing happened. He sent up a thank-you prayer to God—followed not long after by a panicked prayer for God to save his life.

Louie hatched a plan to capture and kill one of the sharks menacing their rafts. Phil would take some bait and dip it in and out of the water to get a shark's attention. As the shark approached the bait, Louie would lean over the side, grab its tail, pull it into the raft, and kill it.

When a five-foot shark approached the bait, Louie was kneeling, ready to strike. He reached over, grabbed the shark's tail, and pulled. He soon learned that a five-foot-long shark was much stronger than a man, at least one hunched over and kneeling in a rubber raft. Instead of pulling the shark into the raft, Louie was pulled overboard. He let out a frantic prayer and leapt from the water back into the raft in a burst of superhuman strength, as if he'd been launched.

When he had calmed down, Louie thought about what had gone wrong with his plan. He concluded that the shark was too big for the raft. Also, he was kneeling too high, making it easy to lose his balance, and he had no plan for how to kill the shark once he hauled it aboard. Louie made some adjustments to his plan. Two days later as some three- and four-foot-long sharks swam around the rafts, he got a chance to try the new plan.

Louie baited a hook with a tiny minnow that had washed into the raft. He handed the bait to Phil, who bobbed it in the water. When a four-foot shark began nuzzling the bait, Louie, staying as low as possible, reached overboard, grabbed its tail, and with a gigantic effort tossed it into the raft. The stunned shark opened its mouth, and Phil jammed an empty flair cartridge into the gaping hole. The shark bit down on the cartridge as Louie grabbed the screwdriver handle of the pliers and plunged it into the shark. The shark thrashed its tail and then was still. Phil and Louie stared at their "catch."

Louie cursed the survival kit for not containing a knife. He would have loved one at that moment. Instead, he pulled out the mirror into which he'd made notches along one edge using the pliers. Louie used this to hack away at the shark's sandpaper-like skin. After ten long minutes, he cut through into the creature's belly. An ammonia-like smell hit his nostrils, causing him to gag. Louie remembered his survival instructor telling him not to eat raw shark meat, since only the shark's liver was good to eat raw. The liver, which took up about a quarter of the shark's body, wasn't hard to find. Louie felt around the dark red, oily organ and soon had chopped it up and divided it among the three of them. The raw shark's liver slid down Louie's throat, reminding him of a hot fudge sundae.

The days adrift slid by. June 17, 1943, marked their twenty-first day in the rafts. Louie believed that it equaled the record set by Rickenbacker and his crew. Rallying his sense of humor, he quipped to Mac, "Now that we've beaten the record, they can come rescue us anytime they want."

Six long, monotonous days later, the distant throb of airplane engines was heard. Louie looked up and saw a bomber in the distance heading away from them. With its twin tail the plane looked like a B-25 bomber. Louie and Phil agreed to use several of their flares and a dye pack to attract the bomber's attention. Louie fired off a flare, aiming it as close to the plane as he could, and then tore open a dye pack and poured it into the sea. He then fired off two more flares while Phil used the mirror to flash the distant plane. But it did no good, and the bomber flew on.

Dejected, Louie slumped to the bottom of the raft. Surely the passing plane must have seen them. Louie's spirits soared when he again heard the sound of airplane engines. The bomber had seen them and was coming back. At last they were going to be rescued. Mac and Phil waved at the approaching plane. Tears welled in Louie's eyes. They had survived twenty-seven days adrift and now were about to be picked up and whisked home to food, water, and solid ground beneath their feet.

The plane dropped low and headed straight for them. All of a sudden its machine guns opened fire. Louie couldn't believe it. The three men rolled out of their rafts into the ocean and ducked below the surface. Bullets exploded across the rafts and into the water. Louie watched the bullets hit the water and then slow down after about three feet and sink toward the bottom. After the strafing, Louie helped Mac and Phil back into a punctured raft and climbed in himself.

"What the heck! Can you believe our guys mistook us for Japanese?" Louie exclaimed as he heard the plane move around for a second pass over them. It was then that he noticed the red circle on the side of the aircraft—it was a Japanese bomber, not an American B-25, as he'd thought.

The bomber came in low again, ready to strafe them once more. Phil and Mac were too exhausted from the first encounter to get back in the water. They both curled up in the bottom of the raft and pretended to be dead while Louie slipped overboard into the ocean. He held a nylon cord so as not to drift away from the rafts. More bullets exploded into the water. Louie could see them tearing holes through the rafts. He knew that Phil and Mac must have been hit many times.

Then Louie was suddenly aware of another danger—sharks. A seven-foot shark swept in at him with its mouth open, teeth bared. Louie opened his eyes as wide as he could and bared his teeth at the shark, just as he'd been trained to do in Hawaii. The shark was unimpressed. It kept coming. When it was within arm's reach, Louie punched it on the snout. The shark retreated.

Louie scrambled back into the raft. Mac and Phil lay there unharmed, not a bullet hole in their bodies. Louie was amazed. He could see bullet holes in the raft all around them. Suddenly he was aware of the Japanese bomber coming back for a third strafing of the raft.

"Just play dead," Louie said to Phil and Mac as he slipped back into the sea.

Once again Louie huddled in the water beneath the rafts, fending off attacking sharks while trying to avoid the rain of bullets. The ordeal was quickly using up every ounce of his physical and emotional energy.

Once the plane had passed and the bullets stopped falling, Louie climbed back into the raft. Again, Phil and Mac had not been hit. And then Louie heard the plane turning for yet another pass.

Louie headed back into the ocean to beat back sharks and avoid the gunfire. But this time there was no gunfire. Louie popped his head up between the rafts to see the bomber drop a black depth charge from its bomb bay. The charge splashed into the water about fifty feet from the rafts, and Louie knew it was the end. At such close range, when the depth charge exploded, he, Phil, and Mac would all be dead. But as Louie beat back another shark attack, he was amazed—the depth charge did not explode. It just sank. Louie supposed that the Japanese bombardier had not armed the charge properly before dropping it. He could hardly comprehend that he, not to mention Mac and Phil, was still alive. How could the rafts be shot full of holes and not one of them be even scratched?

The bomber returned for yet another pass over the rafts. By now Louie was too exhausted to roll back into the water. He just lay down beside Phil and Mac and waited to see what happened. Fortunately there was no more gunfire. The bomber flew over them and then headed west.

Louie surveyed the situation. The raft Phil had been floating in was completely deflated and had been shot in half. Everything that had been in it was lost to the sea. The raft the three of them were now in was punctured in numerous places but had enough trapped air, along with the natural buoyancy of the rubber, to keep them afloat.

The surrounding sharks saw an opportunity. With the raft low in the water they lunged up, trying to grab one or all of the men. The first shark to try this caught them off guard as it landed half inside the raft beside Louie. Instantly Phil grabbed an aluminum oar and beat the shark back into the water. Then another shark did the same thing. By now all three men had oars in their hands and swatted the sharks back.

Louie knew he had to do something to try to save himself and the other two men. The thrashing of sharks over the side of the raft was forcing the raft ever lower in the water. Louie found the emergency air pump, attached it to a valve, and began pumping as hard as he could to get air back into the two tubes that provided the raft's buoyancy. The air came out of the bullet holes a little slower than it was going in from the pump, and the raft began to rise in the water. But the sharks were still thrashing about.

Louie got a system together. One of the men pumped to keep air in the raft, and the other used an oar to beat back the sharks while Louie began repairing the holes in the raft. When the one doing the pumping tired, he would change with the other man while Louie kept patching. However, because Phil and Mac were so weak, Louie would have to take over with the pump for a while to get more air into the raft. But weak as Mac was, Louie was impressed with his ability to swat back sharks.

One by one Louie patched the holes in the raft, cutting back the canvas that covered the punctured rubber with the edge of the mirror, drying the rubber, then roughing it up a little before sticking one of the patches over the hole and holding it in place until the glue stuck. Sometimes a swell would wash across the raft, wetting the patch before the glue dried, and Louie would have to start over. When night fell and Louie could no longer see to patch, the three men took turns working the pump to keep the raft afloat. At first light Louie was back patching until all the holes in the top of the raft were patched. Now he had to come up with a plan to patch the holes in the bottom of the raft.

Since the raft was made up of two separate rubber tubes, Louie let the air out of one tube and then pulled that half of the raft over on top of the buoyant half. Then hole by hole he repaired the punctures. When he was finished, he reinflated the tube and let the air out of the other one to repeat the process. As he worked, Phil and Mac kept watch for marauding sharks. Nearing exhaustion, Louie completed the repair work. He had patched forty-eight holes.

The raft Phil had been riding in was beyond repair. Its yellow rubber coating had been reduced to goo by the relentless sun. But Louie knew that under the rubber were two layers of canvas. Over several days, he slowly pried the canvas and rubber apart with the pliers. Now he had two sheets of fabric. Together they were large enough to provide shade during the day and serve as a blanket at night. It felt wonderful to be out of the direct glare of the sun during the day.

Regrettably, this innovation came too late for Mac, who died on their thirty-third night on the raft, his body completely spent. Louie said a brief eulogy over Mac's body. He was unsure what to say, so he cobbled together a prayer from all the Westerns he'd seen in which one cowboy buried another in the desert. Louie and Phil gently pushed Sergeant Francis McNamara's body overboard. Mac was remarkably light, weighing only about forty pounds, Louie guessed.

They watched Mac's body sink from view. Louie was glad the sharks left it alone.

Now there were just two of them, and if they'd calculated correctly, there was another two weeks or so to go before they hit land. The attack by the Japanese bomber had helped Phil and Louie orient themselves. Given the range of the bomber, the likely time it had set out in the morning, the time it had attacked them, as well as the duration of the attack, Phil decided they must be about 850 miles from land, either the Marshall Islands or the Gilbert Islands. And if that were true, they had drifted about twelve hundred miles west across the Pacific from the crash site of the *Green Hornet*—much farther west than Louie could have imagined.

Rain fell often enough to keep their remaining small canteens full, but there was little food. Louie used his first lieutenant's pin as a fish hook but caught only one fish before the pin was lost overboard. Days blended into one another. Louie and Phil continued to sing, and Louie kept up his three meals a day description routine. But it didn't feel the same. Louie didn't care about food anymore, and Phil stopped correcting him or adding ingredients to the meals. Their appetites had vanished. Louie knew this was the final stage of starvation. They were in the race of their lives—they had to find land before they starved to death.

The men saw encouraging signs as the raft drifted west. The occasional flock of birds flew overhead, and the men heard rumbles in the distance. Louie and Phil also noted specks in the distant sky—airplanes that were too far away to signal. From this they concluded they were getting closer to land—Japanese-controlled land.

On the morning of their forty-sixth day on the raft, a storm began to brew. Clouds hung low and dark, and Louie braced himself for the ride of his life. As the storm approached, Louie knew that neither he nor Phil had the strength to get back into the raft if they were thrown out. He took the length of nylon rope, wrapped it around the inflatable cushion in the middle of the craft, and then wrapped it around his and Phil's waists. If the raft capsized in the storm, they could uncoil the rope around them and cling to it while the capsized raft provided buoyancy. Louie and Phil lay in the bottom of the raft, their legs tucked under the cushion, trying to balance their weight evenly.

Louie soon realized that this was no ordinary storm but a fully formed typhoon. The rain lashed down, and enormous waves, some fifty feet high, swept across the ocean. The raft was lifted high in the air before careening down the other side of the wave. In the trough between one swell and another, Louie bailed water into the raft to act as ballast, keeping it lower and hopefully more stable in the water. As they rode up and down the massive swells, Louie could make out a long, low line in the distance. Phil saw it too—land at last!

As the typhoon became more furious, Louie began to worry about being dashed onto the coral reef surrounding the land ahead. He thought how ironic it would be to be killed by the first piece of land they saw.

All night the storm raged, and Louie was more afraid than when the *Green Hornet* had crashed. He could hardly believe it when the morning finally came. The storm had passed, and he and Phil had survived the fury. They were now drifting toward a line of tiny islands. Soon they were close enough to see coconuts on the trees and thatched huts but no inhabitants. Far above, Japanese Zeros whizzed across the sky.

Louie knew that the Japanese had forced many native populations off their small islands, taking them to larger ones to work as slaves. He hoped that this was one such island. If they lay low, perhaps they could eat fruit and fish and live out the time until the war ended, right under the noses of the Japanese.

That would be something, Louie thought.

But it was not to be. Out of the corner of his eye, Louie spotted a two-masted boat. He froze, then signaled to Phil. Both men began rowing toward land. But they weren't fast enough. The boat turned and sped toward them. Phil and Louie stopped rowing. It was pointless. They couldn't outrun the Japanese boat. As the vessel drew closer, a row of Japanese sailors lined up along the starboard side, each one pointing a machine gun right at Louie and Phil.

Chapter 13

PRISONER OF WAR

Fifteen minutes later, Louie and Phil were each lashed to one of the boat's masts. Their legs too weak to stand on, they had crawled across the deck to get there.

Pow! Louie heard the crack of a pistol butt crash into Phil's jaw. He knew he would be next. Louie braced himself, remembering an old boxing move his father had taught him. Just as the sailor swiped his pistol butt at Louie, Louie flung back his head as if he'd been hit. The pistol missed him, but Louie nearly knocked himself out when his head hit the mast.

Someone who seemed to be the captain appeared and gave orders. The two American airmen were untied and allowed to sit on the deck. Another sailor bowed and brought them a cup of water each and a hard biscuit. Louie bit off a tiny piece and let it sit in his mouth. He sipped some water and felt it wash the food down. He hoped his stomach wouldn't reject it. Eight days had passed since he had last eaten.

Louie had barely finished eating the biscuit when another boat entered the lagoon and came alongside theirs. The sailors pulled the men up and half supported, half dragged them to the railing, where they were lifted over and onto the second boat. The sailors on this vessel didn't attack Louie or Phil but fed them more biscuits and slithers of coconut meat. The trip was short, and soon Louie and Phil were taken off the boat and deposited in a small infirmary.

Louie lay back on the soft mattress covered with a clean cotton sheet. It felt like he was lying on a cloud.

A doctor, who spoke English, entered the room. He examined each man, then helped the men to the scales. Louie weighed around seventy pounds. He had lost over half his already lean body weight while adrift on the raft. The doctor appeared to want to correct this as quickly as possible. He ordered food for the men. Huge quantities of eggs, bread, ham, and fruit salad appeared, and the food was washed down with milk. Louie could hardly believe his luck. Being a Japanese prisoner of war was not going to be so difficult, after all.

A second English speaker, this one an officer, entered their infirmary room. Politely he asked Louie and Phil how they had ended up on the raft, and Louie told him the story. In exchange, the officer told them they had landed on Wotje Atoll in the Marshall Islands.

For the next two days Louie and Phil had everything they wanted: food, medicine, and sleep. On the third day, that all changed. The men were put aboard a freighter that an official said would take them to the nearby Kwajalein Atoll. The official's last words to them were chilling: "After you leave here, we cannot guarantee your life."

Louie and Phil were treated well on the freighter, though Louie felt a pit in his stomach grow every time he thought of what might lie ahead. After twenty-four hours of sailing, Louie was blindfolded, off-loaded from the ship like a sack of potatoes, and thrown onto a flatbed truck. He felt every bump of the short trip. Then Louie was thrown over someone's shoulder again, carried a few yards, and dumped. His blindfold was pulled off, and he saw a Japanese soldier walk out a door. He heard a click as the door locked.

Louie's mind reeled as he tried to grasp where he was. He found himself in a tiny, wooden cell. The floor was the size of a coffin, and the seven-foot high walls supported a thatched coconut frond roof.

It didn't take Louie long to realize he wasn't alone in the cell. As his eyes became accustomed to the dim light, he saw that the floor was alive with white, wiggling objects—maggots! They crawled over his legs and into his salt wounds. Louie recoiled. He tried to swat both them and the flies and mosquitos that were arriving in droves.

For a moment Louie yearned to be back on the open sea in the raft. At least there he could have died with his friend and comrade, and his dignity. Now he had neither. For the first time since his ordeal began nearly two months before, Louie broke down and wept.

At nightfall a guard opened the cell door and grabbed Louie's collar. Louie was still wearing the clothes he'd been "rescued" in, though they were tattered and dyed yellow by the rubber of the raft. The guard pulled Louie around the cell until his head was near the toilet hole. Louie gagged. He had tried to stay as far away from the hole as possible, and now the guard wanted him to sleep with his head right next to it. Louie watched a rat crawling into the bucket below the hole and recoiled. His actions met with a kick. Louie knew there was no point in arguing.

After a long night of scratching mosquito bites and squashing inquisitive maggots, Louie awoke. The guard threw a biscuit into his cell. The biscuit fell apart as it hit the floor. Louie crawled around looking for the crumbs. When he had gathered as many crumbs as he could find, he noticed a tiny cup on the window shelf. He reached up. The cup contained tea, which Louie finished in one gulp. The small cup reminded him of the doll cups his little sisters played with when they were kids.

Louie's digestive system was a wreck, and he knew it. One day, he'd had water and milk and tea to drink, and now there was almost no water. He worried that he would die of thirst after all, especially since he was experiencing a severe bout of diarrhea. He knew he was a prisoner of war and entitled to some rights under the Geneva Convention, so he begged for a doctor. After several days, a doctor arrived at his cell, peered at Louie through the window in the door, and began to laugh. Louie was dismayed. *Don't these people have any compassion?* he wondered. Still, because he knew that someone with diarrhea needed extra fluids or the person would die, he changed his plea from asking for a doctor to asking for more water.

Finally a guard seemed to understand, and Louie watched as the guard stood at the window holding a cup of water. As Louie reached for the cup, the guard grinned and threw the water at him. It was scalding hot. Louie fell back as a blister rose on his cheek. Because even with a scalded face Louie still needed water, he begged again and received the same treatment from the guard.

As Louie sat in his cell day after day, he began to think that he and Phil were the only two prisoners in the place. Sometimes he heard Phil groan or move about several cells down, but he didn't hear anyone else. He did, however, feel like he lived with the ghosts of eleven men. On Louie's wall were scratched the names of eleven Americans who had been captured in the raid on Makin Island in the Gilberts. He knew this because a native of Kwajalein who spoke excellent English had visited his cell one morning and told him so. When Louie asked what had happened to the eleven men, the man gestured with his hand across his throat. "Execution by sword," he said. "They call this Execution Island because no one leaves these cells alive."

The news left Louie wondering why the Japanese were even keeping him alive. He soon discovered part of the answer when he was yanked from his cell and dragged to the porch of a large building. Phil was right behind him. As Louie looked around, his heart sank. Behind Louie were two doctors in white coats, with four men behind them. The men carried clipboards, stopwatches, and a medical bag. In front of the porch a large crowd of Japanese soldiers stood ominously still and stared at Louie.

"Lie down," one doctor said in English. "This is for the good of mankind."

Louie looked up to see a huge hypodermic syringe coming toward him. He tried to squirm, but the assistants held him down.

"Tell us what you feel," the doctor ordered, beginning to inject a green smoky liquid into Louie's arm.

Louie heard a click. He wondered if the stopwatch was recording the last seconds of his life. The porch began to swirl around him. His skin felt like it was crawling with red-hot maggots. His head throbbed. Still the doctor kept injecting him.

"I'm going to faint," Louie cried, and then everything went black.

Louie awoke in his cell, his mouth as dry as cotton, his body feeling like it was on fire. The doctor came to see how he was, and as soon as Louie showed signs of recovery, the experiment was repeated with even more of the green liquid. It was done, yet again, and then on the fourth and final time, an entire pint of the liquid was injected into Louie.

All of this left Louie weak and disoriented. The words of his brother Pete came to him: "If you can take it, you can make it." Louie began to wonder just how much more of this treatment he could take. It was almost a relief when he felt so bad that his mind seemed to float free from his body, the pain too much to bear. Louie was vaguely aware of the doctor visiting him again and using the term *dengue fever*. He had heard of the disease, also known as "breakbone" fever. But whatever it was, it felt good to Louie to be able to leave his body behind and drift into oblivion.

Days passed in a blur, and Louie hardly registered it when groups of visiting Japanese submarine crewmen filed past his cell, spitting at him and throwing rocks and sticks. When they finally left him alone, he became aware that he was bleeding and slimy with spit, but he hardly cared.

After forty-two days on Kwajalein, the unthinkable happened. Louie listened as a group of guards met outside his cellblock and spoke in low voices. Something was up, he knew, but what? Soon an officer pushed the cell door open. Louie held his breath. Was this the end?

"Tomorrow you will board a ship bound for Truk, and from there you will sail for Yokohama, where you will be held as a prisoner of war," the officer announced.

It was hard for Louie to believe it wasn't a trick to lure him from the cell and execute him. But sure enough, on August 26, 1943, Louie and Phil were dragged back to the port and put aboard a Japanese navy ship. During the twenty-one-day voyage Louie imagined all the things being a POW would entitle him to: Red Cross parcels, proper food, medical attention, the right to contact his family and let them know he was safe. Louie had no idea why he and Phil had been spared execution, but as the ship sailed northward, he hoped that the worst of his ordeal was behind him.

Chapter 14

OFUNA

After three weeks in transit, Louie was taken blindfolded from the ship and pushed into a car. He estimated they drove for an hour along hilly, winding roads before stopping. Louie was then led inside and his blindfold removed. He was in a simple bathhouse. In front of him was a tub filled with warm water and disinfectant.

"Get in," a guard said.

Louie willingly stripped off his clothes and sank into the water. It was the first bath or shower he'd had since flying off from Oahu in the *Green Hornet* on May 27. He found a bar of soap and began scrubbing his body. Feeling human again, he almost wanted to sing.

When he got out of the bath, Louie was told to dress again. He'd hoped for some fresh clothes, but the guard pointed his bayonet at the ones he'd just taken off. Louie was concerned. If this was a POW camp, inspected by the Red Cross, why did he have to wear filthy, ripped clothes?

Another guard entered and shaved off Louie's hair and beard. Though on the raft Louie would have loved to get rid of the beard, now he wondered about the coming winter. He hadn't concentrated much on geography in school, but he remembered images of Japanese villages under heavy coats of snow. He had survived the equatorial sun. Was he now going to have to pit his wits against a northern winter? He hoped that this POW camp was well serviced by the Red Cross so that he would have the warm clothing and food he needed.

"You will be meeting an important man now," the guard said. "When you see him, you bow, then you answer his questions."

"Yes," Louie replied, imagining this would be an interrogation.

But what was the point? He had been adrift for forty-seven days, been held captive on Kwajalein for forty-three days, and spent another twenty-one days being transported to this camp. What could he possibly tell the Japanese that would be of any use to them? Still, Louie found himself being led down a dimly lit passageway and into a room. A man in civilian clothes stood with his back to him. Louie bowed anyway and waited.

The man turned slowly, a smile on his face. "Louie," he said, with a perfect American accent. "Do you remember me?"

Louie's blood froze. He was looking into the eyes of Jimmie Sasaki, his friend from USC. "What are you doing here?" he blurted.

Jimmie smiled again and perched himself on the edge of the desk. "Sit down," he said. "You don't look well, and I must say shaving your head hasn't improved your looks either."

Jimmie laughed. Louie was bewildered. This was the kind of bantering Louie had enjoyed when Louie and Jimmie were friends at USC, but not now, in Japan, where Louie was a prisoner of the Japanese.

"I bet you would enjoy breakfast at the student union now. Bacon, sausage, ham, eggs, pancakes . . . ah, I miss American food!" Jimmie said.

The rest of the conversation was one-sided. Louie found it bizarre that Jimmie wanted to relive old times and talk about USC and their mutual friends. Jimmie told Louie that he was a civilian employed by the navy as their chief interrogator. This didn't make much sense to Louie, but then not much that was happening these days did. Louie waited for the first blow to fall, or for Jimmie to ask what he knew about US aviation equipment, but there were no military questions.

"We'll see each other again," Jimmie said as he waved for Louie to leave the room.

A guard waited outside. He led Louie to the courtyard of a compound surrounded by one-story buildings with a high, barbed-wire-topped fence beyond. For the first time since the crash, Louie saw other Caucasians besides Mac and Phil. The sight was jarring. Everyone seemed so tall, but the men's gaunt features and hollow looks told Louie this was no ordinary POW camp. Louie smiled at one airman and greeted him, only to be met with a dull stare.

"Sit there," the guard commanded, pointing to an empty bench. Louie sat. It was cold, very cold, and his shirt had long since lost its sleeves. Louie was dressed for Honolulu weather, not the rapidly approaching Japanese winter.

Everyone stared at the ground until one American, wearing a tattered navy uniform, came over and sat next to Louie. Louie supposed he had permission to do so because the guards didn't rebuff him.

"You are at Ofuna, south of Yokohama," the man said. "It's not a POW camp like you have probably been told." Louie hated hearing his worst fear confirmed. "There's about two hundred of us here. The Allies don't know this place exists, nor do most of the Japs."

"What are we here for?" Louie asked.

"This is a secret interrogation and torture camp. Do your best to follow the rules all the time, even then . . ." The man's voice trailed away.

"What are the rules?" Louie inquired.

"There's lots of them. You'll catch on, but you can start with not looking anyone in the eye. In fact, just keep your eyes on the ground at all times. Don't talk to anyone." Lowering his voice, the American said, "We do use Morse code when the guards can't see us—open hand for dash, fist for dot."

Louie nodded.

"We line up every morning," the navy man added. "The guard makes us count off in Japanese. Better learn to count fast, or they can be brutal. Keep your head down and don't look at anyone or anything. If you need water, you have to ask a guard to let you use the water fountain. There are no cups. And the commander is okay, distant sort of. We call him the Mummy. He looks half dead most of the time. He looks the other way while the guards attack us."

"Oh," Louie said. And as if on cue, he watched a guard smash a man in the mouth with the butt of his rifle. The man buckled and fell to the ground.

"It's hard to get used to how much the Japs hate us personally," the American navy man continued. "It's their culture—they despise anyone who lets himself be taken alive. They think it brings humiliation on the whole family and that soldiers should kill or be killed. There's no room in their thinking for POWs." He shrugged.

Louie's stomach turned as he watched the Japanese guard kick the man on the ground several times and then spit on him.

"Don't try to shield yourself or duck," the American advised. "They hate that too, and they'll beat you harder for it." After a pause he added, "As I said, do your best, but it's pretty unpredictable in here."

Louie was shown to a tiny cell, the sides of which were boards with gaping holes in them; the roof was made of tarpaper. The only things in the cell were three pieces of folded paper and a thin straw mat. Louie soon learned that the sheets of paper were his blanket and the mat was his bed. That night he found it hard to sleep. He longed for a cushion to put under his hips, which jutted into the floor. As he tried to sleep, Louie thought about what he'd seen so far. Judging by the uniforms of the two hundred or so men in Ofuna, most were American airmen and sailors, though he noticed a number of Australian and even some Italian uniforms as well. Louie had scanned the men's downturned faces, looking for someone he might recognize, but he saw no one he knew. The only familiar face had been Jimmie's. Louie was still confused about that.

At six the next morning Louie awoke to a bell ringing and guards yelling, "*Tenko, tenko.*" He knew this meant "line up," and he steadied himself against the wall as he stood. He had no need to dress. He was already wearing everything he owned. Minutes later Louie stood in the prison courtyard alongside the other men. They all bowed toward Tokyo, where Emperor Hirohito's palace was located, and then were dismissed to make a mad dash for the latrines, which the Japanese called *benjo*.

"What happens next?" Louie whispered to the man in the Army Air Force uniform in front of him. Most of the guards had disappeared.

"They're in our cells," the airman replied. "God help you if they find anything. Folding your blanket the wrong way can set them off."

When the guards returned, the men lined up again and marched back to their cells. Soon two Americans walked by carrying a large pot. They ladled a watery rice soup into a bowl. The soup contained what looked like fat grains of black rice. Louie was sure they were rat droppings, and as he held the bowl to his lips, he wondered what diseases they carried.

After breakfast the men were forced to perform tasks such as scrubbing the boardwalks and sweeping the compound. Chores were followed by exercises, which many of the men looked too weak to perform but did so anyway. Anyone who stopped was beaten with a large belt buckle.

Then suddenly there was nothing to do. Because the men were forbidden to return to their cells until nightfall, they stood around in silence. Or at least Louie assumed they were silent, since no one's mouth moved. But when the guards were at the far end of the yard, he heard other prisoners saying "dit dit dit" and "da da da." He looked around. Still no mouths moved. He smiled to himself. They were using short and long sounds made through clenched teeth to give each other messages in Morse code—all without moving their lips.

At nightfall the two American kitchen hands ladled out more slop, and Louie spent another cold night in his flimsy cell. The next morning after roll call, the activities of the day before repeated themselves. Many days passed like this, and Louie tried not to draw attention to himself. The monotony was broken occasionally when Jimmie called Louie in for another "interrogation" session. But all Jimmie seemed to want to do was reminisce and somehow rekindle his friendship with Louie. But Louie would have none of it.

The first snow fell in October, and the trough where the men washed froze over. Louie felt the cold terribly; he was still skin and bone and wore the tattered remains of a tropical uniform. He was grateful when a Norwegian merchant sailor offered him a spare woolen overcoat. Louie didn't know where the man had gotten the coat, but it felt so good he wore the coat twenty-four hours a day.

In November another kind of relief came. No one could figure out why, but the Mummy gave the order that the men could talk quietly to each other while they were outside. This was astounding. For the first time, Louie began to hear detailed accounts of how the other men came to be in Ofuna, and he told his fellow prisoners his own story.

On Christmas Eve Louie thought about his family. He wondered if they were celebrating the traditional Italian Feast of the Seven Fishes. He remembered how much pride his mother took in making fried smelt, anchovy pasta, and octopus salad. The thought of such dishes made his mouth water. He thought about his brother and sisters. Was Pete still alive? Had Sylvia's husband, Harvey, been drafted even though he was a firefighter? And little Virginia. It was shocking to think she was now twenty years old. Was she still living at home?

Christmas Day arrived, and the prisoners of Ofuna were allowed half a Canadian Red Cross package each. Various parcels contained American processed cheese, canned meat and fish, sugar, coffee, milk powder, canned margarine, soap, and cigarettes. Louie knew that each prisoner should have received a whole package once a month, but the guards and the cooks stole most of them. Every few days someone in the camp died from an illness related to malnutrition, and Louie's blood boiled when he thought of the way camp officials stole lifesaving food and other items from prisoners.

On January 26, 1944, Louie turned twenty-seven years old. A month later a newly arrived POW at Ofuna reported that Kwajalein had been bombed beyond recognition and captured by American forces. The news renewed the prisoners' confidence that the United States and her allies would win the war. Louie, like the others, hoped he would live to see the day.

At Ofuna Louie didn't see much of Phil, who was held in another cellblock. In March, Louie and Phil saw each other for a short time. Phil told Louie the Japanese were transferring him to a POW camp named Zentsuji, to which the Red Cross had access. Louie hoped that was true. Phil was dangerously thin and needed better nutrition.

Spring 1944 came, and with it a new challenge for Louie. It was approaching the eighth anniversary of the Berlin Summer Olympic Games, and Louie was a far cry from the strong young man who'd competed in them. Now the officials at Ofuna decided he should race again, this time against a Japanese runner. Louie was aghast at the thought. His legs could barely support his emaciated body, and walking to the benjo required concentration and focus. At first he refused, but prison officials told him if he did not race, the entire camp would be punished. Louie agreed to run.

The Japanese found it amusing to see an American Olympian line up against one of their runners. Almost every guard, along with the prisoners at Ofuna, witnessed Louie and his opponent race lap after lap around the compound. As the race started, Louie was surprised to learn that his body still knew how to run. He ran faster and faster until he realized he had a chance at beating the Japanese runner. He increased his stride, pumped his arms, and sprinted the last lap. The prisoners cheered as Louie crossed the finish line in first place.

Louie stood with his hands on his knees, collecting his breath when he felt a whack on the back of his head. He fell to the ground unconscious. When he came to, several POWs were carrying him to his cell.

"The Japs sure are sore losers!" one prisoner quipped.

Everyone laughed, but underneath they knew it was a serious matter. Louie had nearly paid with his life for winning a race, and bigger stakes were on the horizon. The guards often bragged about their "kill all policy." The authorities in Tokyo had given orders that no POW was to be handed over alive. If the war went badly for the Japanese and it looked like a POW camp was about to be liberated, the guards were to kill all prisoners.

With the arrival of each new prisoner, more news of the war filtered into the prison. The men analyzed every piece of information a new prisoner had to offer. Newspapers were another good source of information. Sometimes someone was able to steal a page from a prison guard's newspaper, and sometimes goods arrived in the kitchen wrapped in newspaper. The pages were all in Japanese, but three men in the camp could read the script, and any pages or scraps of writing were brought to them to interpret.

Not long after the race, as Louie swept the courtyard, he noticed the Mummy taking his morning tea under a cherry tree, frowning and shaking his head as he read the newspaper. Louie concluded something must be going badly for Japan, and he kept sweeping. With every stroke of the broom, he eased a little closer to the Mummy. As the Mummy picked up his teacup, a piece of the paper slipped from his lap to the ground. He didn't appear to notice. Silently, and as slowly as he'd captured the albatross on the raft, Louie reached out with his broom and swept up the piece of newspaper. Still the Mummy did not react. Louie swept the paper over to a corner, picked it up, and tucked it into his shirt. Then he slipped away to show it to his friend Bill Harris, a young marine officer who not only could read Japanese but also had an amazing knowledge of war tactics as well as a photographic memory.

Bill quickly read the page Louie showed him and memorized it. Louie raced the page back to the Mummy, replacing it where it had dropped. That afternoon Bill was able to tell the others what he'd learned. Since winning the battle for Guam a month before, the United States was busy building five airfields there, from which, it appeared, they would launch bombers to attack the Japanese-controlled western Pacific islands and then Japan itself.

Regrettably, Bill had drawn a map he'd seen in the newspaper on a strip of toilet paper. When the camp doctor walked by, he noticed something in Bill's hand.

An investigation took place, and the entire prison population was ordered to line up and forced to do push-ups for twenty minutes. Anyone who faltered was hit in the back or stomped on by a guard. As he labored through the push-ups, Louie wondered what would happen to Bill.

Suddenly the men were ordered to stop and stand at attention. The doctor, whom they called the Quack, grabbed a wooden crutch from a prisoner and with a bloodcurdling scream swung it at Bill's face. Bill stood as the Quack raged at him, kicking and screaming like a madman. Eventually Bill crumpled to the ground, but the beating went on. Louie didn't know how anyone could survive such a vicious attack. Bill lost consciousness, but that didn't stop the doctor. The beating lasted an hour before the Quack walked away, panting from exhaustion.

Two guards dragged Bill away, leaving a pool of blood in the dirt. Louie followed at a safe distance. It was days before Bill could walk again, and when he did, he appeared to be in a daze, unable to remember where he was or to recognize anyone. Louie was devastated to see what had happened to his bright, daring friend. Bill's beating underscored how brutal the Japanese could be, especially as the Allies advanced and captured their territory.

Several weeks passed, and on the morning of Saturday, September 30, 1944, Louie was told he was on the move—to a POW camp named Omori on the outskirts of Tokyo. He had survived one year and two weeks of misery at Ofuna. Louie was grateful to be leaving the place behind, but what lay ahead?

Chapter 15

THE BIRD

L ouie stood at the gates of Omori POW camp with several other prisoners. As he surveyed the gray landscape, his heart dropped. He'd never before seen anything so grim. Omori was a sandy spit in Tokyo Bay. Apart from the oily water surrounding the place, Louie could not see one reminder of nature anywhere—no grass, no trees, no birds, just gray sand and about a dozen long wooden barracks set behind a stockade. A narrow wooden bridge about two hundred yards long connected Omori to the mainland.

"Wait here," a guard ordered.

A minute or so later a corporal stepped from a nearby building. Louie stood to attention. The corporal stared at the prisoners. A minute passed, then two, then five, then ten, at which point the corporal marched over to the POWs, demanding their names.

"Zamperini," Louie said when it was his turn, staring over the man's shoulder. He saw a fist fly toward him. *Bam!* His head reeled back with the punch.

"Why you no look me in eye?" the corporal roared.

Louie stared into the man's eyes. They were cruel and wild.

Bam! A second blow hit Louie's head.

"You no look at me!" the corporal bellowed.

Louie staggered but remained standing. Inside his mind, alarm bells were ringing. What had he come to? Who was this crazy corporal?

Over the next week, Louie learned the answer to both questions. Omori sat on land dredged from the bottom of the bay. It accommodated nine hundred POWs used as slave labor on the docks, loading and unloading ships carrying coal and other industrial supplies. As an officer, Louie did not have to work at the docks. Instead, he and the other officers worked around the camp.

The brutal corporal was Mutsuhiro Watanabe, but the POWs simply called him the Bird.

Some of the men had been imprisoned at the camp for over a year and told Louie stories of the Bird's unbelievable cruelty. The man called prisoners into his office, showed them letters from home, then burned them unopened while they watched. He made the men walk through the overflowing latrine and then lick the bottom of their shoes clean. He offered men candy, then beat them for taking it. He found a book on boxing and lined the men up to practice various punches on them while they stood at attention.

"He enjoys watching us suffer," the sailor on the next bunk told Louie. "God help you if you get on his bad side."

For reasons Louie could never quite fathom, that is exactly what happened. Louie became what the Bird labeled his Number One Prisoner. Louie's every move was watched by the guards and reported to the Bird. Louie encountered the Bird every day and got a beating from him each time.

One guard, Yukichi Kano, was the camp interpreter. He told Louie he was a Christian and would do what he could to help. Louie was grateful. He'd noticed that Kano was different from the other guards. Kano looked the other way when the enlisted men came back from working on the docks and were supposed to be searched. Also, everyone knew that he sneaked into the solitary confinement hut at night, covering any unfortunate soldier with his own blanket, and then returned early in the morning to fetch the blanket before other guards noticed.

Occasionally members of the Red Cross walked through the prison camp doing inspections, but the whole event was staged. The fittest POWs were paraded, and everyone knew the "right way" to answer the questions of Red Cross officials. If a prisoner told the truth about the brutality of the Bird and conditions in the camp, he knew he would be beaten, possibly to death.

The one thing Louie wanted most was to be able to communicate with his family, but this was denied him. He was not registered with the Red Cross as a prisoner of war and was kept out of sight during the infrequent Red Cross inspections of Omori.

Louie's nerves soon stretched to a breaking point. He felt like he was in a constant cat-and-mouse game with the Bird. It was best to keep out of his sight, but this was difficult when the enlisted men left camp to work and only a few officers remained behind. Most days the Bird won, finding Louie and tormenting him.

On November 1, 1944, when Louie had endured a month at Omori, he was performing calisthenics with a group of POWs. A guard stood over them, using his sword to prod any prisoner who did not lift his arms or legs high enough. Suddenly the camp siren went off.

"Into your barracks!" the guard barked.

This was normal, since there were many false alarms at Omori. The men rushed into their barracks, each man not wanting a beating for being the last man in. Louie stood staring out the barracks window, listening. There it was, the thrum of large airplane engines.

"It's ours!" someone yelled jubilantly.

The men, Louie among them, stampeded for the door. In the courtyard Louie stared up at the underbelly of the largest bomber he'd ever seen. On the plane's side was painted the familiar blue circle with a white star inside.

"What is it?" someone yelled.

"Has to be the B-29 Superfortress," a newly arrived POW shouted back.

The men started to chant, "B-29! B-29!"

"Get back inside," a guard shouted.

No one moved. It was worth risking a beating to see an American bomber flying over Japan.

The B-29 did a final loop and headed south as the prisoners returned to their barracks to discuss what they'd seen. The newest POW told them what he could remember. The B-29 was an advanced bomber. It had a pressurized cabin, allowing it to fly high, and remote-controlled machine-gun turrets. Louie was particularly interested in its size: it had a wingspan of 141 feet and was 99 feet long. A B-24's wingspan was 30 feet shorter, and the fuselage was 33 feet shorter.

"No wonder they call it a Superfortress," Louie commented.

The appearance of the American bomber gave Louie hope that he would be rescued, if he could just survive the Bird's brutal treatment. The Bird's latest tactic was to beat Louie about the head with his huge belt buckle, gently tend to his wounds, and then beat him with the buckle again in the same place. One such attack left Louie temporarily deaf in his left ear.

In mid-November the Bird brought two Japanese men dressed in civilian clothes to Louie's barracks.

"We have something to show you," one of the men said, handing Louie a piece of paper.

Louie started reading: "Transcript of NBC Radio Show, November 12. USA." The paper went on to say that Louis Silvie Zamperini, who had been missing at sea since May 27, 1943, had now been declared dead by the United States War Department. Louie frowned as he read. Why would these two men want him to see this?

"Wouldn't you like your family to know the truth?" the second man asked.

"Of course," Louie replied, looking for the trap.

"Come with us. We are the producers of *Postman Calls*, an English-language production of Radio Tokyo, which corrects mistakes such as this one."

Louie had heard of this Japanese propaganda station. It tried to demoralize American troops by spreading rumors and half-truths about what was going on in the fighting.

"I'll have to ask my superior officer if I can," Louie said.

"Very well. Let the corporal know when you are ready, and we will come to get you."

Louie spoke to the ranking Allied leader of the Omori camp, General Maher, and learned that various other POWs had been given the opportunity to broadcast over *Postman Calls*. Louie decided to do the broadcast.

Two days later Louie was driven to the radio studio in Tokyo, where he was allowed to read over the air a short speech he'd written. He began, "Hello, Mother and Father, relatives and friends. This is your Louie talking . . ." He went on to talk about how he was still alive and to mention as many names of fellow POWs at the camp as he could.

When it was over, the men congratulated him.

"Your voice was made for radio!" exclaimed one.

"Wouldn't you like to send messages home whenever you liked?" asked the other. "Wouldn't you like your parents to be able to hear your voice on the radio every week?"

Louie began to feel uneasy. "Can I write my own scripts?" he asked.

Both men shook their heads. "No, we have already written what you will read," Louie was told.

Louie was then given a piece of paper, which he read quickly. The script didn't even sound like him, and it criticized the United States and made it sound as if the Japanese were looking after him well.

"I can't read this," Louie said, handing the paper back.

"Think carefully," the taller of the two men said. "You could stay here at the station, eat in the cafeteria every day, sleep in a guest room with crisp cotton sheets, and speak to your family and friends."

"Not like that," Louie said. He was adamant that he would not become a propaganda tool for the Japanese.

"You think about it," the other man said. "You don't do this, and you go to punishment camp."

Louie's heart dropped. He thought he was in one of those already.

When Louie got back to Omori, he waited for news that he was being shipped to a punishment camp. Instead something surprising happened. The Bird left! It was one of the happiest days of Louie's life. He was free from the madman who had tried to destroy him. Now Omori was a much better place. Not getting beaten every day felt marvelous.

Each day now B-29 bombers appeared in the skies above Omori. Sometimes the men watched full-on dogfights between them and Japanese Zeros trying to stop the B-29s from reaching their targets. Louie felt frustrated looking up at the dogfights. He'd trained so hard to be up there and would have given anything to bomb the Japanese at that moment.

As the weeks passed, more bombing took place over Japan. In mid-February 1945 the bombs began falling early in the morning.

This was a wonderful sign. Since bombers typically didn't fly through the night, the prisoners surmised that they must be launching from a giant aircraft carrier, which had to be nearby. The Allies were closing in on victory.

In all the excitement, Louie almost forgot the threat of punishment camp, but on March 1, he and several other officers were marched out the gates of Omori for the last time. Their destination was Naoetsu on the west coast of Honshu Island and about one hundred miles northwest of Tokyo.

As the men traveled by truck and train for two days across Honshu, a winter storm descended across Japan. Snow fell, blanketing the land, and by the time the men reached their destination, drifts were fourteen feet deep. The men were ordered off the train and prodded at the end of a sword to walk through the snow the one and a half miles to the camp, located at the confluence of two rivers near the edge of the Sea of Japan. The camp consisted of a large, barnlike, two-story wooden building whose few windows were heavily barred. Louie was numb with cold by the time he entered the prison camp gates.

"Stand and wait," their guard said, leaving the men in front of a low, ramshackle hut beside the barracks.

The men waited and waited. The cold crept under Louie's coat and squeezed the air from his chest. Suddenly the door of the hut flew open and out stepped a man Louie recognized instantly. It was the Bird.

"O God," Louie prayed as he steadied himself against the shock. He knew he could endure many things, but another round with the Bird? He wasn't sure he would survive that.

Louie soon discovered how bad the punishment camp was. The temperature dropped below zero the first night. A contingent of emaciated Australian soldiers, who had been there the longest, explained that they had pulled up many of the floorboards to burn for heat. Now the snow drifted in under the two-story barracks, and it was colder than an icebox.

Gradually Louie and the new arrivals were told horror stories about the camp. Sixty shoebox-sized boxes were piled against the wall. Louie learned that each box held the ashes of a POW who had died. Rats rustled among the boxes at night, gnawing their way inside and scattering gray ash everywhere.

Just as before, the Bird pursued Louie mercilessly. Louie wondered if the Bird had specially requested he be transferred to Naoetsu so he could continue his torment of him.

The standard protocol at the Naoetsu prison camp was that officers did not work. But as winter receded and ice on the Ara River beside the camp melted, Louie and the other officers were hitched to wagons carrying human waste and told to pull them six miles to a farm. The work was backbreaking, though not as backbreaking as what was to follow.

In April 1945, the Bird decided the officers should unload coal off barges into railway cars bound for the nearby steel mill. The baskets of coal each man carried from the barge up the riverbank to the train car weighed about sixty pounds, and the prisoners were prodded into working at a furious pace. When a barge was emptied, it was towed with the men aboard out to a coal ship anchored offshore. In the heaving sea, the prisoners were ordered to jump across to the ship, grab the rope net draped over the vessel's side, and climb up and board the ship.

Louie, like many of the men, now suffered from beriberi and was unsure of his balance. That didn't matter. Everyone was to jump from the swaying barge onto the side of the ship. Louie made it successfully. In the hold of the ship, he took his place shoveling coal into a net that was hoisted from the hold and dumped onto the barge. If Louie or any of the other prisoners stopped work, even for a moment, they were clubbed on the back of the head with a kendo stick. The backbreaking work left the men covered from head to foot in grime. Once every ten days Louie got a bath, but between baths he became as black as the coal he shoveled for fourteen hours a day.

Day after day, week after week, Louie and the others attacked huge mounds of coal, knowing that when they conquered them, another ship would slip into the bay and their labor would begin again.

In the spring, Louie fell off a narrow ramp while carrying a heavy basket of coal on his back. As he hit the ground, he knew something was wrong. Unable to walk on his own, he was taken back to camp, where he lay in a pall of black soot. His ankle and knee burned with pain, and he knew he had torn some muscles. Because it was impossible for Louie to return to the dock to work, the Bird found a special job, just for him.

Louie was put in charge of a single pig in the camp. Each day he had to feed it and clean its sty—with his bare hands. Louie felt fresh waves of revulsion every time he crawled around the sty, scooping up handfuls of pig dung and mud. His mind whirled with the list of diseases he was exposing himself to, but there was no alternative. He prayed every day that the war would end.

In May 1945, the men at Naoetsu got some good news and some bad news. The bad news was that four hundred more men were marched into their camp—to share their already meager food supply. The good news was that these men had fresh information, and the news was momentous. The men had come from Kobe and Osaka, both strategic Japanese cities, and both had been bombed and completely burned. The Allies were systematically destroying Japan's

largest cities. The men brought other astounding news too. In early
May, Germany had surrendered. The war in Europe was over! It was
only a matter of time before the Allies beat the Japanese. The POWs
at Naoetsu had to hang on and wait.

Just as in Tokyo, the prisoners noticed American B-29 bombers
flying over the town. And as the planes flew over, the men's treatment inside the camp grew worse. One day the Bird made all the
officers line up and ordered each enlisted man to punch every officer
in the face, hard. Two hundred twenty punches later, Louie and the
other officers were bloodied, their faces turned to pulp. It was days
before Louie could open his mouth enough to mumble a few words.

The Bird and his fellow guards did all they could to break the
POWs, reminding them that they would never leave Naoetsu alive,
no matter how the war went. Already stories of Allied prisoners being
slaughtered by their Japanese captors in other POW camps across the
Pacific and Southeast Asia had filtered into camp from arriving prisoners. Fear gripped the men at Naoetsu.

When, on August 6, 1945, Louie noticed the guards were particularly angry and violent, he wondered what had happened. Then a
POW reported that a Japanese civilian at the dock had insisted that
the city of Hiroshima had been destroyed, not by many bombs from
B-29s, but by a single bomb.

A single bomb destroying the second largest city in Japan? It
didn't seem likely. None of the POWs had any idea the United States
had a bomb that powerful. Three days later, word reached the camp
that a second bomb had been dropped, destroying the city of Naga-
saki. Again the POWs gathered in groups trying to figure out what
had happened.

Louie was not among them. He lay on his bed, sick with beriberi. The disease was caused by a lack of vitamin B1, and without

medicine he knew he would be dead by the end of the month. Above the camp he was vaguely aware of B-29 bombers flying overhead. The end seemed so close, and Louie willed himself to hold on.

August 20, 1945, was a day Louie knew he would remember. The commander ordered all the prisoners to assemble in the courtyard. Someone helped Louie to his feet, and Louie shuffled out the door and lined up. The Bird, who had brutalized Louie during his waking hours and at night in his dreams, was nowhere to be seen.

The camp commander marched from his hut and spoke in Japanese. An interpreter translated his words. "The war has come to the point of cessation."

It took a second for the words to sink in. The war was over! Or was it? Louie, like everyone else, stood silent. Was it a trick, one last cruel joke before they were all executed? Louie waited tensely.

"You may bathe in the river," the interpreter told the men.

The men moved nervously toward the gate. Two of Louie's friends linked their arms in his and helped him along. Louie was standing naked in the water when the first B-29 buzzed them, its lights blinking.

"That's Morse code!" someone yelled. "It says, W-A-R O-V-E-R."

Louie and the rest of the men went wild. They had heard it from the Allies. The war was over, really over, and soon they would be going home!

Chapter 16

DREAMS AND NIGHTMARES

A nyone got a great story? Anyone got a great story?"
Louie ignored the man standing at the train station in Yokohama. Still weak and emaciated from his ordeal, he'd been told that in the Red Cross building just a few yards away was enough coffee, Coca Cola, and donuts for all the POWs who had just arrived on the train. Heading for the building, Louie felt a friend grab him by the shirt.

"This guy has an incredible story!" his friend yelled at the reporter.

The reporter blocked Louie's way. "What's your name?" he asked.

"Sorry, I have to get to the donuts," Louie replied, trying to squeeze past.

"Hold on, tell me your name."

"Louie Zamperini, and I have to get to the Red Cross building," Louie said.

The blood drained from the reporter's face. "Louie Zamperini? That's impossible. He's dead."

"No I'm not! I know who I am. I'm Louie Zamperini," Louie snapped.

"Can you prove it? Do you have ID?" the reporter asked.

Louie sighed. "Look, I just want a Coke and a donut, okay? Nothing personal. Maybe we can talk after I've had some food."

"I can't print a story like this without proof," the reporter insisted.

Louie reached into his pocket and pulled out his wallet. The Japanese had taken everything except a USC pass with Louie's name on it.

The reporter stared at the pass, then at Louie. "Hey," he yelled to another reporter on his left. "Get this guy some food, will you?" He turned back to Louie and introduced himself. "I'm Robert Trumbull with the *New York Times*. Step over here and tell me about the crash."

Over the next hour Louie told the reporter the entire story. Trumbull's eyes grew wider with each new revelation. By the time he had finished talking, no one had brought Louie food, and POWs coming off other trains had eaten everything the Red Cross had to offer. Louie would have to wait for the next meal.

The trip home for Louie was long. He was transported by plane to Okinawa and on to Guam, the Philippines, and finally Hawaii, where he was hospitalized to gain weight. In Hawaii, Louie learned that Allen Phillips (Phil) had also survived. Louie hadn't seen Phil since he was transferred from Ofuna to another POW camp a year and a half earlier.

On the way to Hawaii, Louie had been given a red pamphlet written for returning airmen. It began, "Good? Bad? Mixed up? Or can't you tell? That's O.K., though. It's exactly how thousands of men have felt who have come back ahead of you. Some of them wanted to talk it over. But some of them didn't even want to think about their feelings . . ."

The pamphlet then centered on a returning airman named "John Brown." Louie read about John Brown's ups and downs, his attempts to fit in while feeling strangely isolated from the people around him, and the ways he tried to get help. The story concluded, "No matter how much help John Brown got, though, in the final analysis it was up to him. The real, permanent solution, he found, *lies with the individual man himself.*"

Louie smiled and nodded. The pamphlet's message was true. He'd been through so much in the two and a half years since the *Green Hornet* had crashed, surviving on his wits and iron determination. He felt sorry for the John Browns of the war, men who would struggle to get on with their civilian lives. Louie wasn't going to be one of them. He had plans to run in the next Olympic Games and had dreams of success, driving a fast car, partying, and making up for lost time.

On October 2, 1945, Louie arrived in San Francisco to receive more treatment for the tropical diseases he'd developed as a POW. Then in mid-October, General Hap Arnold sent a B-25 especially to fly Louie, along with his brother Pete, who'd joined him in San Francisco, on the last leg of his journey home.

Louie looked out the window as the B-25 prepared to land at Long Beach, California. His stomach knotted as the bomber made its final approach. On one hand he couldn't wait to see his parents and sisters. On the other hand he couldn't think of what to say to them. They would never understand what he'd been through, the terrible things he'd had to witness and do. He couldn't begin to tell them about the Bird, even though the cruel guard haunted Louie's dreams every night.

The Zamperini family was on the tarmac waiting for Louie. Louise Zamperini engulfed her son in an enormous hug as he stepped from the plane. Louie relaxed. He was home. Everything would be fine.

Just as after the 1936 Olympics, it seemed the entire town of Torrance turned out to welcome Louie. Chief John Strohe was there in a patrol car, lights flashing, and the high school cheerleaders waved pom-poms. Louie remembered how great it felt coming back after the Olympics. He had been the fastest American in the 5,000 meters and had many funny stories to tell. Coming home as a former POW felt different, however. Everyone called him a hero, but what, Louie pondered, had he done that was heroic—besides survive?

At the Zamperini home on Gramercy Street, Louie dutifully ate the cake Virginia had baked and answered questions from the reporters crowded into the house. When the reporters left, Louie's mother nodded. The family left the room and returned a minute later laden with colorful packages.

"We never forgot a birthday or Christmas," his mother said, wiping away tears. "We bought you something every time. We knew you'd come back and open them."

Louie opened one brightly colored gift after another. There were phonograph records and even an expensive record player.

When all the gifts were open, his sister Sylvia smiled broadly. "One more thing," she said, reaching for a record and placing it on the turntable of his new player. She set the needle onto the record, and a woman's voice began to speak. "Hello Mother and Father, relatives and friends. This is your Louie talking . . ."

"Stop it! Stop it! Take it off!" Louie yelled. He was shaking all over and cursing as Sylvia leapt up and turned off the record player.

"Smash it! Smash it to smithereens!" Louie shouted.

With tears in her eyes, Sylvia snapped the record in half. "Whatever you say, Louie," she said timidly.

Louie stood and stomped upstairs to his old bedroom. He slammed the door and lay down on the bed. The next morning he apologized to Sylvia.

"We just thought you'd like to hear it," Sylvia said. "Mother and Daddy listened to it every day. It's an announcer reading your message. It's how we knew you were alive."

"I know, I know," Louie answered. "It's just not something I want to be reminded of—ever."

Truth was, Louie was trapped with the memories of being a POW. In his waking moments everyone wanted to hear from him. Two thousand people wrote wanting to know if he'd seen their son or husband, others asked questions about his time on the raft, and many invited him to speak at schools, at clubs, or on the radio. Louie was overwhelmed. He felt he had to say yes to every speaking invitation. But each time he spoke he was vividly reminded of his terrible ordeal, first at sea, then in the hands of the Japanese. Even in his sleep he couldn't seem to escape. Each night the same images rose up in his dreams—the Bird beating him with a stick, the Bird telling him he would die soon, the Bird forcing him to lick filth off his shoes. On and on the images came, until Louie would awake in a ball of sweat and hatred.

It didn't take Louie long to decide that alcohol was his best hope for blunting the memories. At first Louie drank only before he gave a speech. Then he started drinking earlier, until he was reaching for a bottle of whiskey at breakfast—*just enough to smooth my entrance into a new day,* he told himself. Drinking at night also held the promise of help. Louie drank long into the evening, hoping the nightmares would not haunt him in a drunken stupor. But they did.

One problem Louie didn't have was money. The army paid him $10,000 in back pay, and the life insurance company let him keep the $1,600 it had paid to his parents when it was believed that Louie had died. Louise and Tony Zamperini had put every penny of the life insurance money in the bank for Louie, believing he was still alive.

Five months after returning to Torrance, Louie was off to New York City to fire the starting gun at a track meet in Madison Square Garden. The event had originally been called the Zamperini Memorial Mile, but when Louie was found to be alive, the name was changed to the Zamperini Invitational Mile.

From New York Louie flew down to Miami Beach for a break. Returning servicemen were given two weeks of rest and relaxation, and Louie decided to take his in Florida. In Miami Beach, he got up to his old tricks. There was a fence along the beach that cordoned off an expensive private club called the McFadden-Deauville Club. Louie had never seen a fence he couldn't scale and was soon on the other side, strolling toward the bar. After a couple of cocktails, he turned to see a young woman with long blonde hair and a dazzling smile walk through the room. The woman didn't even glance at Louie, but he couldn't think of anything else. *A woman like that,* he thought, *could take a man's mind off any nightmare.*

The following day Louie jumped the fence to the club again. This time he headed for the beach, where, to his delight, he found the same woman sunbathing with a friend. Her name was Cynthia Applewhite, and she was happy to chat with Louie. Soon Louie learned she was the only daughter of a wealthy family.

As they talked, Louie realized their childhoods could not have been more different. She had gone to the best private schools, while he had scraped his way through public school. She had servants at home and ate off fine white china with silver cutlery, while he had sat around a big white table eating fast to get his share of seconds. She traveled first class on trains; he had jumped trains and ridden in freight cars with hobos. They also discovered their birthdays were just six days apart, hers on January 20, his on January 26, though she was twenty and Louie was twenty-nine. The age difference didn't matter to Louie. He found Cynthia warm, easy to talk to, and beautiful.

Within a week Louie had done something he couldn't have imagined: he told Cynthia he loved her. He knew his behavior was impulsive, but with the golden sunset, the white sand, and palm trees swaying in the cool evening breeze, it seemed like the right thing to do.

Louie was relieved when Cynthia didn't laugh at him. Instead, she canceled her list of social engagements so that she and Louie could spend the second week of Louie's vacation together. By the end of that second week, they were talking of marriage. While Cynthia was sure that her parents would hate the idea, she was equally sure that marrying Louie was what she wanted. When it came time for Louie to leave, the couple set a wedding date for August and agreed that Cynthia should visit Louie soon in California.

Cynthia arrived in May 1946, and Louie took her home to meet his parents. Things did not go well. Cynthia was shocked at the small, clapboard house Louie had grown up in, and she had trouble understanding his father's Italian accent. Louie said he'd take her back to the airport if that's what she wanted, but she said she would continue her visit.

When newspaper reporters got wind of Louie's engagement, they followed him and Cynthia everywhere. The *Los Angeles Times* printed a photograph of the two with the words "Will they jump the gun?" below it.

That is what Louie and Cynthia did. Deciding they could no longer wait to be married, they gathered up Louie's family on May 25, 1946, and said their marriage vows at an Episcopal church in Los Angeles. After a small reception, Louie took his new bride to the nearby Chatham Hotel.

"I just want to call my mother and tell her what we've done," Cynthia told Louie at the hotel.

Louie frowned and uncorked the magnum of champagne he planned to share with Cynthia.

Meanwhile, Cynthia dialed the number. "Hello, Mother," she said, then burst into tears.

Louie listened as his wife tried to explain to her mother why they had married in such a hurry.

"Just hang up and call her again in the morning," Louie said, gulping down a glass of champagne.

An hour later Cynthia was still pleading for her mother to understand, the magnum of champagne was gone, and Louie was drunk. He went to bed alone. As he drifted off to sleep, the Bird arose once again in his dreams to crack Louie over the head with his belt buckle.

Chapter 17

FINALLY HIS WAR WAS OVER

I'm sorry," the doctor said, wrapping Louie's ankle in a bandage. "You're never going to run hard on that ankle again. The muscle will keep tearing. There's just too much residual damage."

Louie clenched his fists, fuming inside. It was six months since the wedding, and he had taken up running again. He was doing so well, until now, when the injury he had sustained falling off a plank while carrying a heavy basket of coal at Naoetsu POW camp resurfaced. His hope of running in the 1948 London Olympic Games was gone—stripped away from him by the Bird and his cadre of cruel guards.

As he drove home, Louie became more agitated. Wasn't it enough that he jumped at the sound of a slamming door, that every night he had to get drunk to steel himself for the nightmares, that his wife told him she was embarrassed by his behavior? Wasn't that all enough, without the Bird taking away his Olympic chances as well?

Over the next weeks, rage grew in Louie's soul until it was all he thought about. He knew what he had to do, what would bring him peace. He would make enough money to go back to Japan, hunt down the Bird, and kill him with his bare hands as he looked directly into his eyes.

Louie threw himself into his new goal. The faster he made money, the faster he could return to Japan and kill the Bird. He and Cynthia were living in Hollywood, and there was no shortage of people wanting to steer Louie toward various postwar, get-rich-quick schemes. Louie tried them all. He invested in an Egyptian movie, an earthmoving equipment company in the Philippines, a fishing licensing scheme in Mexico—he even considered hiring himself out as a mercenary! Nothing lasted. Nothing made him money. Nothing made him happy.

After about two years, all Louie's money was gone, and the Zamperinis found themselves living in a tiny, dark apartment, their car about to be repossessed, their marriage in tatters, and a baby on the way. Louie still couldn't bring himself to seek regular work—he had to find a way to make big money so he could go to Japan and end his nightmares. He'd hardly thought it possible, but the nightmares seemed to be getting worse. A recent nightmare was so vivid, so horrific, that Louie awoke straddling Cynthia, his hands firmly around her neck, terror in her eyes. He couldn't blame her for being terrified. He was shocked as well. He didn't sleep anymore that night, pondering what would have happened if he hadn't woken up.

During the day, the Zamperini home became more violent. Tensions mounted as Cynthia's dream of a loving husband and beautiful family faded. Louie came home one day to discover that Cynthia had smashed her perfume and lotion jars on the floor. Another time she slapped Louie, and he hit back. It was not a good environment for a baby, but on January 7, 1949, Cynthia Battle Zamperini, Cissy for short, was born.

Louie was enchanted with his little daughter, who had blonde hair and big blue eyes, just like her mother. But even a beautiful baby couldn't distract Louie for long from his nightmares. Nothing, he was convinced, had the power to stop the nightmares, except killing the Bird.

The tension at home got worse, and one day Cynthia came home to find Louie in a rage, shaking baby Cissy. That was her breaking point. She told Louie that living with a war hero was one thing, but living with a man who could not put that war behind him was quite another. She wanted a divorce. Louie completely understood.

Several days later Louie stood in the hallway of their apartment complex fuming. The new neighbor who'd moved in was unbelievable. All he wanted to talk about was Jesus. Jesus healed him. Jesus was his best friend. Jesus talked to him. Louie decided the man was completely crazy, but when they passed each other in the hallway, Cynthia was polite enough to listen to him. And now the man was inviting her to a tent meeting at the corner of Washington Boulevard and Hill Street in downtown Los Angeles. A young southerner named Billy Graham was preaching at the meeting. The neighbor said he'd drive Louie and Cynthia there. Louie walked away.

Several minutes later Cynthia came into the apartment. "I'm going tonight," she announced.

Louie rolled his eyes and reached for a bottle of whiskey.

The Cynthia who left the apartment that night and the Cynthia who returned were two different people. Louie could see it immediately. Cynthia announced that she was no longer interested in divorce, that she would pray for Louie until he found the peace of Christ in his heart, just as she had at the Billy Graham Crusade meeting. Louie couldn't believe it. He was relieved that the divorce was off, but the religious stuff was shocking. He'd married a smart, self-reliant woman and ended up with a holy roller! It couldn't be. But it was. Cynthia and the neighbor nagged Louie relentlessly, until he agreed to go to one of the tent meetings. Louie told Cynthia that after that she was not to talk about religion ever again at home.

Louie and Cynthia stood outside a huge tent erected for the event. Louie read the sign draped on the front of the tent: "Greater

Los Angeles Crusade, 6,000 free seats!" Inside the tent Louie sat down as close to the exit as possible so he could make a quick get-away. Someone stepped on stage and started singing a hymn. Louie didn't know the words. A second hymn followed. Then the huge crowd hushed as the preacher walked in. Billy Graham was not at all what Louie expected. He was young, younger than Louie, and he had movie-star good looks and spoke with a southern drawl.

"Please open your Bibles to the Gospel of John, chapter eight," Billy said.

Louie watched as Cynthia flicked through the Bible the neighbor had given her.

Billy began to read from the passage, "Jesus went up unto the mount of Olives . . ."

Louie looked around. Of the twenty people in the row in front, eight of the men and five of the women were wearing black shoes. Louie kept looking around, desperately trying to distract himself from hearing anything the preacher said. But occasionally snippets of the sermon penetrated his mind. He heard Billy talk about how God would judge every person who ever lived. "He will use His holy standard, and many people will hear the words 'Depart from Me, I never knew you.'"

Louie wanted to jump out of his seat and crack Billy Graham on the jaw. How dare he say that! Louie was a good man, a kind man, a faithful man. God would never tell him to depart from Him.

"Here tonight, there's a drowning man, lost in the sea of life," the preacher went on. The life raft flashed through Louie's mind. How many times had he prayed to God during that perilous time, believed that God would help him, promised God that he would serve Him?

"Now with every head bowed, and every eye closed, you can raise your hand, signifying that you understand you're a sinner and that you want to invite Jesus Christ to be Lord of your life."

Louie grabbed Cynthia's hand. "Let's go," he said, jerking her out of the seat and racing out of the tent.

Tears slipped down Cynthia's cheeks as they drove home in silence.

The next morning Cynthia started encouraging Louie again. "We should go back tonight, Louie. If you just do what Mr. Graham says, you'll find peace. I know you will."

Louie knew one thing for sure: he never, ever wanted to go back to a tent meeting again. He refused to go. But Cynthia wouldn't give up.

"All right," Louie finally gave in. "If you can find a babysitter, and as long as we leave before all that 'every eye closed' stuff, I'll go."

Listening to the second sermon, Louie found it harder to distract himself. Billy quoted the Bible again: "For what shall it profit a man, if he shall gain the whole world, and lose his own soul?"

Louie didn't like to think about his soul, or anyone else's for that matter, but Billy went on. "When you receive Jesus as your Savior, you are regenerated by the Spirit of God. Your life is transformed. You are a new person in Christ. Remember, Jesus doesn't want part of your life. He wants all of your life. He wants you to repent of your sins and then completely and totally surrender your life to Him and follow Him."

This was too much for Louie to take in. How could a person give up his whole life? What would that mean for him? No more parties, no more nights drinking, no more fun—ever again. What would he do all day? And at night, if he was totally sober, how would he handle the terrible nightmares that came?

"You may not think you can lead a good Christian life," Billy said, "but Christ will help you."

Louie eyed the nearest exit. Sweat poured down his face, and he was having trouble breathing. He had to get out of there.

"Nobody is leaving now," he heard Billy say. "This is a sacred time. Everybody be still and quiet. Let the Holy Spirit work in your heart."

Louie looked over the rows of bowed heads and bolted for the exit. He heard Cynthia behind him.

Halfway up the aisle, Louie stopped. He could go no farther. He remembered the raft and his prayer: "God, if You get me out of here, I will seek You and serve You forever." And now here he was, running from God as fast as he could. But why was he running? His life was a disaster. He was exhausted, jobless, penniless, worn-out. Why was he ashamed to say he needed Jesus Christ to lift him out of it all?

Slowly Louie turned around and walked back down the aisle, not to his seat this time, but to the prayer room, where he knelt and prayed. There for the first time he poured out his heart to God—no bargaining, no excuses, nothing held back. At that moment Louie did not feel like an Olympian or a war hero. He was only profoundly grateful that he was just another sinner who needed forgiveness.

When Louie got up off his knees, he knew something was different. He felt light, forgiven, cleansed from the inside out. But he felt something else too, something unexpected. The hatred he'd harbored for so long for his Japanese captors, even the Bird, was gone, completely gone.

That night when he got home, Louie poured his bottles of liquor down the drain. He didn't think twice about it. He didn't want to drink from them anymore. He also threw his cigarettes into the trash.

Louie went to bed that night sober and fell into a deep sleep. When he awoke the next morning, it took him a moment to register what had happened. He had just spent the first night in over four years free from a nightmare about the Bird. Louie started to weep. It was over. His war was finally over. Billy Graham was right: he was "a new creation in Christ," and the old had passed away.

Chapter 18

FORGIVENESS

I'm going out for a while," Louie told Cynthia a couple of days later. "I'm going down to the Veterans Employment Services to apply for work."

Cynthia beamed.

As he drove downtown, Louie thought about his past attempts to make money—it had never been about getting a job or bringing home a regular paycheck. Now he felt different. He was sure he'd get some kind of work through the Veterans Employment Services. The work might not be glamorous, but it would provide honest money to take care of Cynthia and Cissy. Perhaps if they saved hard, they might be able to buy a tiny house one day.

When he had gone forward at the Billy Graham Crusade meeting, Louie had filled out a follow-up card, on which he had listed his name, address, and phone number. The day after his trip to the Veterans Employment Services, Louie was contacted and asked to visit Billy and his choir director, Cliff Barrows, at the tent downtown. Louie shook hands with Billy and Cliff, and Billy asked Louie to describe what had happened to him. Louie was pleased to do so, and he had some questions of his own. He'd noticed he wanted to spend a lot of time alone at the park or in his apartment reading the Bible and thinking about his life. Was that normal?

Billy assured him it was. "God's bringing things to the surface so He can deal with them. He's renewing you from the inside out."

After a pause, Billy said to Louie, "This has been an amazing week. Two other well-known men, Jim Vaus, who works for the mobster Mickey Cohen, and Stuart Hamblen, the entertainer, also accepted Christ this week. Cliff and I have been praying about it, and we want you to think about joining us and giving your testimony on stage."

Louie shook his head. "Not me. I'm getting a regular job. I want to be a regular Christian. I don't want to be in the limelight anymore. I've left that behind."

"Pray about it," Billy said, putting his hand on Louie's shoulder. "All I'm going to ask you to do is to pray about it."

Two weeks later, Louie was on a train to Modesto, California. Cliff Barrows had bought the ticket and asked Louie to speak at the church where his father was pastor. "Just tell your war story, and the raft story, and then what happened when you came forward in the tent. You can do that, can't you?" Cliff had said.

Louie had to agree that it didn't sound difficult. And it wasn't. Because Cliff's father's church had recently burned down, Louie gave his talk and then his testimony in a large tent. He enjoyed the experience.

The three high-profile conversions at Billy Graham's Los Angeles Crusade caught the attention of the media. Suddenly Louie's story, along with those of Jim Vaus and Stuart Hamblen, was being splashed over the pages of the *Los Angeles Times* and *Life* magazine. Like it or not, Louie was back in the spotlight. In fact, Louie never did take up a regular job. Instead he accepted speaking requests up and down the West Coast. Because by now his car had been repossessed, he took the train to the various venues, or one of his new Christian friends drove him.

Life for Louie was different now. He prayed before he made

decisions and asked God to help him pay his bills. And it all worked out. Most of the places where Louie spoke took up an offering for him, allowing him to use that money to meet his family's expenses and eventually buy a replacement car. Louie was careful to give 10 percent of anything he received back to Christian ministry.

The Zamperini family flourished. They were poor, but happy to have found peace at last. Louie marveled at how he could ever have been taken in by all those get-rich-quick schemes. Money didn't seem that important anymore. Following God did.

During the summer of 1950, Louie was asked to give his testimony at a Christian conference being held at Winona Lake in northern Indiana. A huge crowd came to listen to the many missionaries and evangelists who gathered there every summer to exchange stories and encourage one another. Louie found the conference atmosphere inspiring. Before he became a Christian, he had no idea such gatherings even existed. Now he enthusiastically participated, at least until he heard Bob Pierce speak.

At first Louie liked Bob's talk. Bob was a rugged man who'd traveled around Asia conducting Christian crusades and filming the hardship children faced after the war. Louie remembered seeing children with protruding stomachs, wide eyes, and ragged clothes in Japanese villages at the end of the war. Bob talked about raising money to help these children, but then he said something else. "Why are we American Christians so focused on sending missionary teams to Europe? Hundreds of teams are headed over there, and rightly so, but what about Japan? Don't you think Japan needs missionaries too? General MacArthur called for twenty-five thousand missionaries to be sent there, and no one has gone. How can that be?"

Louie wasn't sure, but he didn't want to think about it too deeply. All he knew was that he was done with Japan. As soon as Bob finished speaking, Louie slipped out the back of the meeting hall. He wasn't in the mood to talk to anyone.

As he walked back to his hotel room, Louie couldn't shake the idea that he was supposed to not only go back to Japan but also visit the prison at Sugamo, where he'd read that all the Japanese war criminals, including a number of guards from POW camps, were being held.

"God," Louie prayed as he walked, "You know I don't want to do that, so if You want me to go to Japan, please make it very clear. I'm a new Christian. You'll have to give me a swift kick in the pants so that I know it's really You."

Halfway across the conference grounds a stranger walked up to Louie. "Hi, I'm Eric Folsom," the man introduced himself. "I heard you give your testimony earlier. Would you be willing to speak at my church in Tucson?"

Louie breathed a sigh of relief. For a minute he had thought the man was going to ask him about Japan. "Sure," he said, reaching into his pocket and pulling out a business card.

"By the way," Eric continued. "Did you hear Bob Peirce's challenge about Japan?"

"I did," Louie replied and then changed the subject. "Give me a call when you get home, and we'll arrange a date for me to visit your church."

"Bob's message was quite something, wasn't it?" Eric persisted.

"Yes, it was," Louie said. "Well, I'm off to my room," he added, stepping away from the conversation.

"Hold on," Eric said, putting his hand on Louie's arm. "Since we've been talking here, God has impressed me to give you $500 toward your ministry trip to Japan."

Louie's heart sank. There was no escaping it. He had to go back to the land of his old nightmares.

"I don't have the money on me," Eric went on. "I'm going to have to sell my car to raise it, but that's okay. God will provide. I'll send you a check in a week or two at the latest."

Louie was humbled. He knew how hard it was to be without a car, and this stranger was ready to sell his in order to get him to Japan. It was the kick in the pants that Louie couldn't ignore.

Barely an hour later Louie heard a knock on his hotel room door. He opened the door to find six young people standing in the hallway. A young woman stepped forward and said, "Mr. Zamperini, we were touched about the challenge to go to Japan and decided you would be the best person to go." She held out an envelope. "This money is for you"—Louie stared blankly as the young woman went on—"to help you get there."

Louie mumbled some thanks, shut the door, and sat down on the bed. How had his world turned upside down in the course of an evening? He'd been going along fine, giving his testimony, praying with Cynthia, reading his Bible, and now this? He was perplexed. Did he really want to see those prison guards again? What if it tipped him over the edge? Louie hadn't had a single nightmare since accepting Christ at the tent meeting, but would that change if he actually stood in a prison again or stared into the eyes of the Bird? It was a huge risk, and Louie knew it as he wiped sweat from his face.

In October 1950, Louie was sitting aboard a Northwest Airlines plane heading out across the Pacific. The aircraft would stop over at Honolulu, then Wake Island, before going on to Tokyo. Louie was familiar with all three places. The flight itself was pleasant enough, though Louie's heart was in turmoil. On the one hand, he wished he hadn't come, but on the other hand, he was sure it was God's will for him to be going.

Louie had no guarantee he would even be allowed into Sugamo

Prison. Hardly anyone was, but he had to try. On his arrival in Tokyo, several men from *Life* magazine's Tokyo bureau approached Louie at the airport. They had been tipped off that he was planning to go to Sugamo and asked Louie if he could get passes for them too. They'd been trying for months to get into the prison. Louie promised he would try.

It felt surreal to Louie to once again be in Japan. A busy itinerary awaited him. A group of pastors and chaplains had put together a schedule that included Louie speaking at many American army bases, universities, and churches. Wherever he went to speak, Louie was well received, even though he spoke honestly about how brutal some Japanese guards had been to him and the other POWs.

One night Louie was scheduled to speak at Tokyo's newly erected civic auditorium. Despite heavy rain that night, twenty-three thousand people showed up to hear him. In the end he had to give two back-to-back talks to accommodate everyone. Louie was astonished and humbled by the response.

So far in Japan, Louie had not met anyone he knew. He wondered whether doing so would make a difference. He would find out soon enough.

It had taken a lot of negotiating, but in the end, General Douglas MacArthur himself gave Louie, along with reporters from *Life* magazine, permission to visit Sugamo Prison. Louie braced himself as he made his way to the prison in Tokyo. It felt strange as he walked through the prison gates. He was now a free man, able to walk in and out as he pleased, while many of his former guards were now the prisoners. Once he would have been gleeful at the thought, but now he was sobered by it.

A guard escorted Louie into a large room, where over eight hundred men sat on the floor awaiting his arrival. According to the escort, they were all former prison guards and were housed together so they could attend their hearings at the ongoing war-crimes trials.

As he stood to speak, Louie scanned the audience. He didn't recognize anyone in the front few rows, but then he spotted familiar faces farther back—the Quack, Jimmie Sasaki, and several others. He kept looking, but he could not see the Bird.

Louie found giving the talk about his experiences surprisingly easy. As he looked out on the sea of confused faces, he felt waves of compassion for these men who had made his life and the lives of countless other prisoners of war a living hell.

When the talk was over, the men who knew Louie were invited to come to the front and meet with him. It was the moment Louie had dreaded, being face-to-face with his former tormentors. But as the men started to file forward, their heads down, Louie found himself running down the aisle. He threw his arms around the first man, looked him in the eye, and told him that God loved him and so did he. Louie's compassion grew with every one of his old guards he saw. It was a wonderful and amazing moment for him as he realized his faith in God had truly changed him.

As he was escorted from the prison, Louie had just one question: Where was the Bird?

"We've spent a lot of money and resources looking for him," Louie was told. "He is number twenty-three on our most-wanted list, but recently we have had information that he killed himself."

Louie felt sad—sad that the Bird had been that desperate and sad that he did not have the opportunity to tell the Bird he forgave him.

On the return trip to the United States, Louie couldn't help smiling. He'd made new friends and spoken about his faith. But more than that, he had faced the worst circumstances of his life head-on and had come through the experience unshaken.

Chapter 19

RESURRECTED

Louie didn't slow down upon his return to the United States. He was more in demand as a speaker than ever. Now when he spoke, he included his experience at Sugamo Prison. Louie's favorite audience to speak to was young people who had lost their way. He spoke to kids in youth camps and prisons, detention centers and foster homes. He would start by telling them what it was like to be a prisoner of war, to lose your dignity, to then be consumed by so much hate and rage that your only purpose in life became returning to the place of your humiliation and murdering someone. This got the kids' attention! Louie then gave them ways they could break out of their situations and take responsibility for their own actions. He explained how he had become a Christian and how running had given him a healthy focus when he was a boy.

Louie knew firsthand that sports had the power to distract young people and set them on a different path. After three years of thinking about it, Louie decided to set up his own youth program, which he called Victory Boys Camp. He found a dilapidated campsite in the San Gabriel Mountains outside Los Angeles and set to work making the place fit to occupy.

Meanwhile, the Zamperini family had moved into their own small house, and a second child, a son named Louis Jr., was born on August 4, 1953. Cynthia and Louie called him Luke.

When the work of restoring the camp was finished, Louie, along with two other Olympians he had enlisted, took thirty-five boys up into the mountains. Some of the boys were convicted felons and gang members, and Louie had to be deputized before the police released them into his custody. Louie wasn't concerned. He believed that underneath, these boys were scared and confused. They needed direction, and what better place to find it than alone in nature?

Louie led treks into the mountains, where he taught the boys survival skills along with rappelling, horseback riding, and primitive camping. At night, when the boys were exhausted, Louie told them stories around the campfire. He told them about the Bird and about how easy it was to be consumed by hate and injustice. Then he told the story of his return to Japan, sharing how his bitterness was washed away and he experienced such eagerness to embrace his old foes. Louie knew that what the boys needed most was someone to be honest with them about how hard life could be and how they could get through it. He was grateful for every terrible situation he'd lived through when he thought about how his experiences could help the boys.

Louie's life was full. He loved working with the boys camp and raising his own two children.

In early 1954 Louie got a big surprise. He had gone to a television studio for what he thought was a simple interview. As he walked onto the set, he heard an announcer's voice: "Louie Zamperini—THIS IS YOUR LIFE!" That night Louie was the subject of a popular television show that surprised its guests with events and people from their past. Cynthia sat on a couch holding Cissy on her lap. Behind Louie stood his parents. One by one people walked out from backstage to greet Louie and tell a story about him. Jesse Owens was there, as was Louie's old USC coach. And Phil, his pilot, life-raft mate, and fellow POW survivor during World War II, came from Indiana to be on the show. He'd driven there himself, swearing he would never fly again.

At the end of the show, the host presented Louie with a gold watch, a movie camera, a Mercury station wagon, and a check for $1,000, which Louie used to help fund his Victory Boys Camp.

Following the television show, New York publisher E. P. Dutton asked Louie to write his autobiography. They paired him with a ghostwriter named Helen Itria. The result was the book *Devil at My Heels*, published in 1956. Louie was given an $8,000 advance for the book, which he used to buy a house in the Hollywood Hills. Once again, demand for Louie to tell his story in person grew, and he accepted as many speaking invitations as he could while still running his boys camp.

As the years passed, Louie and Cynthia maintained a busy life. With the children getting older, Louie supplemented the family income by buying and selling commercial real estate in Los Angeles. He also helped run a program for the elderly at his church and taught Bible class.

As the years changed to decades, the Zamperinis traveled from time to time, but Louie didn't go back to Japan. That changed when he was invited to run the Olympic torch through Naoetsu on its way to the 1998 Nagano Winter Olympic Games in Japan. Louie didn't have to think twice about accepting the invitation.

On July 26, 1998, his eighty-first birthday, Louie dressed in a blue-and-white tracksuit and was ready and eager to run the one-kilometer leg of the journey holding the torch high. It was a rainy day, and thousands of Japanese children wearing brightly colored raingear lined the route, cheering him on. Louie knew that the grandchildren of his former tormentors and guards could well be among those waving their flags so joyfully at him. It was a magical moment, unimaginable fifty-three years before when he had been imprisoned just half a mile away.

When the torch was passed to the next runner, Louie was taken to visit the site of the former POW camp where he had been imprisoned. It was a beautiful place now, a Peace Park, with two towering statues representing Peace and Friendship. Louie marveled at the story of the park's founding. The people of Naoetsu had banded together to buy the land and turn it into a memorial for the Allied men who had been imprisoned, worked, and died there. They were the first community in Japan to honor the men who had been captured and abused. Louie gazed up, his eyes wet with tears. Once he'd tried so desperately to forget this place. Now he prayed he would always remember it.

Louie enjoyed watching the Winter Olympic Games. He particularly looked forward to the closing ceremony. The CBS television network had spent the past two years producing a thirty-five-minute movie about his life called *The Great Zamperini*. It was to be played to the gathered crowd and also broadcast worldwide. Louie had helped with the movie, combing through boxes of old letters, papers, and photos to help the scriptwriters. At the same time, a producer had gone to Japan to research what had happened to Louie's prison guards. No one was more shocked than Louie to learn that the Bird was still alive! The producer even interviewed Mutsuhiro Watanabe on film, but Mutsuhiro refused to meet with Louie in person. Louie was disappointed. He had imagined how wonderful it would have been to wrap his arms around the Bird and tell him he forgave him.

Following the 1998 Olympic Games in Nagano, another flurry of interest in Louie arose. Louie traveled when he could, but he soon learned that Cynthia had cancer. His world stopped as he cared for his ailing wife, who died on February 21, 2001, at the age of seventy-five. They'd been married for almost fifty-five years. As Louie looked back, he was grateful that she had pushed him to go to the

Billy Graham Crusade meeting. It had not only rescued him from the ugly pit he was in but also saved their marriage.

In 2002, Louie received a letter that began, "Dear Mr. Zamperini, My name is Laura Hillenbrand, and I am the author of a new book, *Seabiscuit*." Louie knew all about Seabiscuit, a small racehorse, who against the odds became a champion. Seabiscuit had been a powerful symbol of hope to many Americans during the Great Depression. In the letter, Laura explained that in her research for the book, she had read many sports pages from the era and had seen the name Louie Zamperini many times. She had read some of the articles on Louie and promised herself that when *Seabiscuit* was released, she would research Louie's life more thoroughly. Now, she told him, she wanted to write his story.

Louie was not enthusiastic. He'd just finished rewriting and updating *Devil at My Heels* with David Rensin. The updated autobiography included many new facts discovered during the making of *The Great Zamperini*. Still, Laura persisted. She pointed out that this would be a biography, quite different from his telling of his story. She would be able to include stories of his friends after the war and interesting facts about what was happening during the war in other places. This was not possible in an autobiography. Louie was hooked by the approach. He believed that Laura could tell his story through fresh eyes for a new generation. He and Laura talked on the phone, and Louie offered to help her in any way he could. He later realized it was one of the best decisions he ever made.

On January 26, 2007, Louie turned ninety years old and was just as active as ever. One of his favorite things was visiting the marines at Twentynine Palms Marine Corps Air Ground Combat Center to teach them about combat survival. It reminded him of his time in Hawaii when an old native man taught him how to fend off an attacking shark. Louie told the marines the story with a chuckle. "Pay attention," he said. "You never know when you might need to remember this."

Louie engaged in other activities, many of which scared his children. When the trees around his hillside home needed to be trimmed, Louie took on the challenge, climbing them, chainsaw in hand. He also still liked to ski, not on the bunny slopes but on the double diamond runs, swooshing around flags and reveling in the speed and grace of it all.

To honor his birthday, Louie's family and friends arranged a charity dinner at USC, with the proceeds going to his beloved nonprofit Victory Boys Camp. At the dinner it was announced that a statue of Louie would be placed in what was already called Zamperini Plaza, outside the university's track stadium. An annual award would also be presented to the most inspirational athlete on the USC track team.

Louie loved the dinner, and he was in fine form when he spoke. "I can't keep doing this," he quipped. "Too many birthdays can kill you." Then he added on a serious note, "There's not a person in the world I'd trade my life for, even with everything I've been through."

The year 2008 was particularly tough for Louie. He became a different kind of survivor, the one who survived the deaths of his siblings. In May his brother Pete, who'd introduced him to running and set his feet on a different path, died of cancer. Two months later his sister Virginia passed away, and in October Sylvia died. Louie, who himself had a death certificate dated 1943, had outlived them all.

Two years later, in 2010, *Unbroken: A World War II Story of Survival, Resilience, and Redemption* was published. Because of Laura Hillenbrand's ongoing poor health, it had taken her eight years to research and write the book. The result was well worth the wait. The book shot to the top of the *New York Times* bestseller list and was hailed as the top nonfiction book of the year by *Time* magazine. The *Wall Street Journal* described it as "Extraordinarily moving . . . a powerfully drawn survival epic."

In 2011, when ninety-four-year-old Louie realized that Laura would not be well enough to launch a book tour, he volunteered to do it. He was back on the road again. Over the next twelve months Louie spoke at nearly fifty events as he crisscrossed America. He even visited the Billy Graham Center in North Carolina, where he saw an exhibit of the 1949 Los Angeles Crusade. In Washington, DC, he met Laura in person and thanked her for bringing his story back to life. He joked that she had resurrected him.

There was more to come. In 2012 Angelina Jolie read *Unbroken* straight through—twice—and then determined to direct a movie about Louie's life. She struck a deal with Universal Studios, the Coen brothers collaborated on the script, and British actor Jack O'Connell was signed to play the film's lead role. Louie was hired as a consultant for the film, a role he relished. He particularly liked the way Angelina summarized the point of the movie: "In the end, its message is one we all need now more than ever—the journey of a man finding his way through the darkness and into the light."

Louie could hardly wait to see the movie, which was to be released on Christmas Day 2014. But in late May 2014 Louie got pneumonia. Ninety-five years earlier, the same illness had sent his parents on a cross-country journey to save Louie's and Pete's lives. The two brothers had thrived in California. Now Louie was battling the fight of his life. He fought on for forty days before he died peacefully in his sleep at his Hollywood Hills home on July 2.

Tributes and honors poured in after his death. The mayor of Torrance ordered all flags in the city flown at half-mast to mark a week of mourning for the Torrance Tornado. A private funeral was held for Louis Silvie Zamperini on July 13, 2014, at Hollywood Presbyterian Church. A public memorial service followed two weeks later at Torrance High School.

Torrance did her favorite son proud. Over two thousand people turned up to honor Louie in the school stadium that bore his name. Members of the Torrance High School track team ran a symbolic lap in his honor, and World War II–era planes flew overhead in the missing-man formation. Tears were shed, but for the most part it wasn't a sad occasion. "He had ninety-seven years of a life well-lived. We mourn him. But we also celebrate him," Louie's son Luke told a local reporter.

Even as Louie was buried, the movie *Unbroken* was undergoing postproduction and final editing for release five months later. Louie Zamperini would live again on the big screen, inspiring a new generation with one last chapter in his amazing, improbable, and victorious story.

BIBLIOGRAPHY

Barnard, Bonnie Mae. *Old Torrance, Olmsted Districts.* Charleston, SC: Arcadia, 2006.

Boyington, Gregory "Pappy." *Baa Baa Black Sheep.* New York: Bantam Books, 1977.

Brown, Daniel James. *The Boys in the Boat: Nine Americans and Their Epic Quest for Gold at the 1936 Berlin Olympics.* New York: Viking, 2013.

Hillenbrand, Laura. *Unbroken: A World War II Story of Survival, Resilience, and Redemption.* New York: Random House, 2010.

Hymans, Richard. *The History of the United States Olympic Trials—Track & Field.* N.p.: USA Track & Field, 2008.

Kiell, Paul J. *American Miler: The Life and Times of Glenn Cunningham.* Halcottsville, NY: Breakaway Books, 2006.

Lobb, Charles; foreword by Louis Zamperini. *Torrance Airport.* San Francisco: Arcadia, 2006.

Wade, Tom Henling. *Prisoner of the Japanese: From Changi to Tokyo.* Kenthurst, NSW, Aust.: Kangaroo Press, 1994.

Zamperini, Louis. "Louis S. Zamperini 1936 Olympic Games Track & Field." Interview by George A. Hodak. Los Angeles: Amateur Athletic Association of Los Angeles, 1988.

Zamperini, Louis, with David Rensin. *Devil at My Heels: A Heroic Olympian's Astonishing Story of Survival as a Japanese POW in World War II.* New York: Perennial, 2003.

Zamperini, Louis, with Helen Itria. *Devil at My Heels: The Story of Louis Zamperini.* New York: Dutton, 1956.

Movies:

The Great Zamperini. CBS Sports, 1998.

Zamperini: Still Carrying the Torch. Billy Graham Evangelistic Association,
    1992.

Archives of the *Los Angeles Times*, *New York Times*, and *Torrance
    Herald* newspapers were also consulted.

ALSO FROM JANET & GEOFF BENGE...

More adventure-filled biographies for ages 10 to 100!

Heroes of History

Abraham Lincoln: A New Birth of Freedom • 978-1-883002-79-4

Alan Shepard: Higher and Faster • 978-1-932096-41-5

Ben Carson: A Chance at Life • 978-1-62486-034-8

Benjamin Franklin: Live Wire • 978-1-932096-14-9

Billy Graham: America's Pastor • 978-1-62486-024-9

Captain John Smith: A Foothold in the New World • 978-1-932096-36-1

Christopher Columbus: Across the Ocean Sea • 978-1-932096-23-1

Clara Barton: Courage under Fire • 978-1-883002-51-0

Daniel Boone: Frontiersman • 978-1-932096-09-5

Davy Crockett: Ever Westward • 978-1-932096-67-5

Douglas MacArthur: What Greater Honor • 978-1-932096-15-6

George Washington Carver: From Slave to Scientist • 978-1-883002-78-7

George Washington: True Patriot • 978-1-883002-81-7

Harriet Tubman: Freedombound • 978-1-883002-90-9

John Adams: Independence Forever • 978-1-883002-50-3

Laura Ingalls Wilder: A Storybook Life • 978-1-932096-32-3

Louis Zamperini: Redemption • 978-1-62486-050-8

Meriwether Lewis: Off the Edge of the Map • 978-1-883002-80-0

Milton Hershey: More Than Chocolate • 978-1-932096-82-8

Orville Wright: The Flyer • 978-1-932096-34-7

Ronald Reagan: Destiny at His Side • 978-1-932096-65-1

Theodore Roosevelt: An American Original • 978-1-932096-10-1

Thomas Edison: Inspiration and Hard Work • 978-1-932096-37-8
William Penn: Liberty and Justice for All • 978-1-883002-82-4

Christian Heroes: Then & Now

Adoniram Judson: Bound for Burma • 978-1-57658-161-2
Amy Carmichael: Rescuer of Precious Gems • 978-1-57658-018-9
Betty Greene: Wings to Serve • 978-1-57658-152-0
Brother Andrew: God's Secret Agent • 978-1-57658-355-5
C. S. Lewis: Master Storyteller • 978-1-57658-385-2
C. T. Studd: No Retreat • 978-1-57658-288-6
Cameron Townsend: Good News in Every Language • 978-1-57658-164-3
Clarence Jones: Mr. Radio • 978-1-57658-343-2
Corrie ten Boom: Keeper of the Angels' Den • 978-1-57658-136-0
Count Zinzendorf: Firstfruit • 978-1-57658-262-6
D. L. Moody: Bringing Souls to Christ • 978-1-57658-552-8
David Bussau: Facing the World Head-on • 978-1-57658-415-6
David Livingstone: Africa's Trailblazer • 978-1-57658-153-7
Dietrich Bonhoeffer: In the Midst of Wickedness • 978-1-57658-713-3
Elisabeth Elliot: Joyful Surrender • 978-1-57658-513-9
Eric Liddell: Something Greater Than Gold • 978-1-57658-137-7
Florence Young: Mission Accomplished • 978-1-57658-313-5
Francis Asbury: Circuit Rider • 978-1-57658-737-9
George Müller: Guardian of Bristol's Orphans • 978-1-57658-145-2
Gladys Aylward: The Adventure of a Lifetime • 978-1-57658-019-6
Hudson Taylor: Deep in the Heart of China • 978-1-57658-016-5
Ida Scudder: Healing Bodies, Touching Hearts • 978-1-57658-285-5
Isobel Kuhn: On the Roof of the World • 978-1-57658-497-2
Jacob DeShazer: Forgive Your Enemies • 978-1-57658-475-0
Jim Elliot: One Great Purpose • 978-1-57658-146-9
John Wesley: The World His Parish • 978-1-57658-382-1

John Williams: Messenger of Peace • 978-1-57658-256-5

Jonathan Goforth: An Open Door in China • 978-1-57658-174-2

Klaus-Dieter John: Hope in the Land of the Incas • 978-1-57658-755-3

Lillian Trasher: The Greatest Wonder in Egypt • 978-1-57658-305-0

Loren Cunningham: Into All the World • 978-1-57658-199-5

Lottie Moon: Giving Her All for China • 978-1-57658-188-9

Mary Slessor: Forward into Calabar • 978-1-57658-148-3

Nate Saint: On a Wing and a Prayer • 978-1-57658-017-2

Paul Brand: Helping Hands • 978-1-57658-536-8

Rachel Saint: A Star in the Jungle • 978-1-57658-337-1

Rowland Bingham: Into Africa's Interior • 978-1-57658-282-4

Samuel Zwemer: The Burden of Arabia • 978-1-57658-738-6

Sundar Singh: Footprints Over the Mountains • 978-1-57658-318-0

Wilfred Grenfell: Fisher of Men • 978-1-57658-292-3

William Booth: Soup, Soap, and Salvation • 978-1-57658-258-9

William Carey: Obliged to Go • 978-1-57658-147-6

Heroes of History and Christian Heroes:
Then & Now are available in paperback, e-book,
and audiobook formats, with more coming soon!
Unit Study Curriculum Guides are available
for many biographies.

www.HeroesThenAndNow.com
1-800-922-2143